CHILDREN'S LONDON

by

Caroline Brakspear
and
Helen Mann

THE DAILY TELEGRAPH/THORNTON COX

CONTENTS

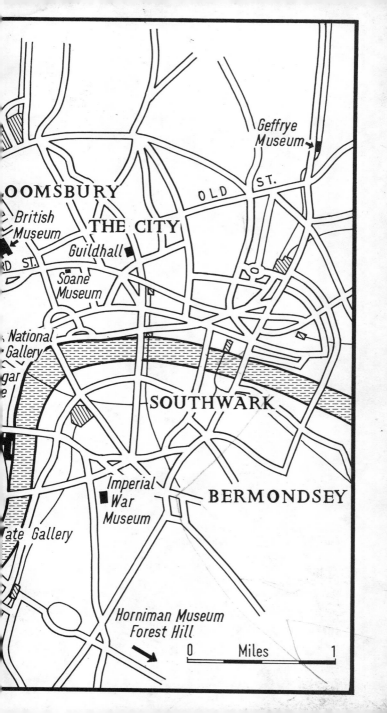

Published by Thornton Cox Ltd. and distributed by
Tom Stacey Ltd., 28 Maiden Lane, London WC2E 7JP

Printed by Simpsons of Newbury Ltd., Berkshire

Maps and drawings by Anne Colvin and Zbigniew Karbowski.

SBN 0 902726 09 9

INTRODUCTION

Our children have enjoyed helping to compile this guide, but were jealous of the time we spent crouched over our typewriters. My daughter Kate says that she cannot think why I am taking so long to write this introduction. "Just say that everything in London is interesting and fun, especially eating". She is not alone in her attitude. Every other child we talked to rated 'eating out' high on the list of favourite city pastimes. "But you can't eat all day long", I protested weakly to one of Kate's nicest greedy friends. "I definitely can", replied Lucy indignantly and proceeded to prove it. Well, almost. I did walk them the long way round between restaurant, cafe and icecream parlour. Mercifully for one's pocket and figure, other activities came out top of the popularity poll too.

We have tried to include them all, together with the information which you will need to find them, arrive at the right time, and not miss out on anything along the way. We have given the name of the nearest tube station to help you get your bearings and have included all the entrance fees and charges payable. We must point out that these are all subject to alteration with the coming of VAT, and that, at the time of going to press, most organisations had not decided their new prices. Either check before you go, or be prepared to pay a small additional charge. Telephone numbers are listed so that you will not waste time thumbing through your directories.

Helen's two children, Alexandra and Justin, are 13 and 11. Mine, Rupert and Kate, are 10 and 8. With them, and dozens of their friends, we have had plenty of guinea-pigs to practise our ideas upon. Helen and I both work part-time, so we were not just concerned with jaunting about giving them treats, but wanted to find out what was available to them which would provide an outlet for all their energy and creativity and give us some free time into the bargain. The holidays are a great time for children to learn a new sport or to experiment with some new art or craft which they may not learn at school. So we have searched for art and theatre workshops, clubs, sports organisations and community and play centres which would help provide what they are looking for.

We went sightseeing and investigated countless museums and monuments. We have tried to give you some of the historical background too. As we explored the city we discovered certain facts. One was that so long as the adults enjoyed themselves, so did the children, but that at the first sign of adult boredom, the complaints department would go into action and suddenly everyone's feet would be tired. The younger ones often adored doing things which on the face of it were totally unsuitable for them. Two toddlers had a great old time scooting about on their amply padded bottoms whilst we enjoyed a culture-vulture afternoon at the Tate with some older children. They did not disturb anyone, and though we cannot swear that they appreciated the pictures, they certainly looked at some of them with interest and the rest of us had a glorious time. With this age group we came up against one of London's weaknesses. There are not enough lavatories about. When there was not a public one or a department store nearby, we resorted to dashing into the nearest shop and pleading for help. It works, but we suspect there is an element of blackmail to the method.

We realised that there is a definite limit to the amount of time that children can concentrate in museums and galleries. It seemed to be a case of little and often until they became really engrossed in one particular subject. They all needed to dash about and let off steam afterwards. Novelty was one of the greatest entertainments of all. Children who were used to being ferried about in cars were knocked out by travelling in buses and on the underground. We began to think that we would become a permanent fixture on the Circle Line as we indulged this passion. The bus-hopping that a Red Rover allows was extremely popular too; it hardly seemed to matter where they were going, so long as they could keep getting off one bus and onto another. We encouraged the older ones to go about by themselves, but as every family has different ideas about when a child is responsible enough to cope alone, we leave that up to you.

We spent long days rusticating in the parks and enjoying London's river. We took picnics and paddled and fished and made houses in hollow trees. We played scavenger, laid trails, made maps, watched the birds, flew our kites, and generally lazed about. All the children were very environment conscious and one of the most popular games was to imitate the Wombles and clear up litter. We explored the riverside, trailing along the towpaths, beachcombing and joining the riverboats when we could afford to. Altogether we have had a marvellous time discovering the many delights that London has to offer children and we hope that this book will help you to do so too.

One word of warning, all the prices we've quoted are pre—VAT, so be prepared to pay a little more in some cases.

Caroline Brakspear

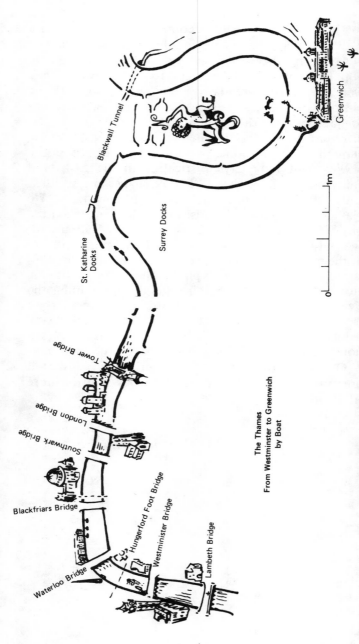

St. Katharine Docks

Blackwall Tunnel

Greenwich

Surrey Docks

Tower Bridge

London Bridge

Southwark Bridge

Blackfriars Bridge

Hungerford Foot Bridge

Westminster Bridge

Lambeth Bridge

Waterloo Bridge

0   1m

The Thames
From Westminster to Greenwich
by Boat

4

THE RIVER

The Thames is the reason for London's existence. The Romans chose this site because of the hill rising from the marshy swamps and because the river here was narrow enough to bridge. Since then, ships from all over the world have sailed up the Thames to trade their cargoes and so make the Port of London one of the greatest in the world. It is very much a working river with the docks stretching for miles downstream from the Tower to Tilbury. Cranes dominate the skyline and tugs drag their flotillas of laden lighters upstream. Once, the Thames was London's main thoroughfare; it was often easier to travel by boat than to try to negotiate the crowded narrow streets. This would probably still be the case but no-one has yet provided a sensible river bus. All the most important buildings were built close to the river; palaces, Parliament, the Tower, the great churches and the markets were grouped within a stone's throw of the water. The Lord Mayor's Procession was staged on the river, and it must also have been a splendid spectacle when the great State Barges swept by, carrying the King and his Court to the country calm of the palaces at Richmond, Hampton Court, or Greenwich. There was only one bridge until 1750, so the river was thronged with watermen ferrying people across.

London Bridge must have been an extraordinary sight, lined as it was with houses, and with its grisly fortified gates decorated with the decapitated heads of traitors. Until it was demolished in 1832, its nineteen arches formed a barrier to the tide and during very hard winters the river froze. Then there would be all the fun of the Frost Fairs, with booths and sideshows set up on the ice. There were barbecues too, and in 1683 the ice was so thick that they managed to roast an ox on the river. In summer the river could be very unpleasant. It was used as a sewer and gradually became so foul that in 1858, after a very hot summer with little rain, the smell was so awful it was known as the Great Stink and it was at last decided something had to be done to provide an alternative sewage system. What with the sewage and the industrial waste that came later, the fish which used to provide many a Londoner with a free meal disappeared. Now, as pollution is being tackled, some are beginning to return, though probably salmon will never again make their marvellous leaping dash to the spawning grounds upstream. People cannot swim in the river either; the water is still so disgustingly dirty that they would be almost certainly dragged off to hospital and the stomach pump if they even fell in. Quite apart from the filth, the current is very strong as the river is tidal, so be very careful if you decide to go beachcombing at low tide. (Definitely a 'permission first' outing in any case). But the river is there to explore by boat or towpath, with both town and country on its banks. There are four interesting boats to examine at their moorings; museums and palaces to east and west, and boat races to watch.

BOATS TO EXAMINE

HMS Discovery moored at Victoria Embankment, WC2 01-240-2639

Tube: Temple. Open daily except Christmas Day 1.00-4.30p.m.

Scott's Polar Research Ship now belongs to the Admiralty, and is a museum containing relics from his Antartic voyages.

HMS Belfast moored at Symon's Wharf, Wine Lane, Tooley Street, SE1. 01-407-6435

Tube: London Bridge. Open daily except Christmas Day 11.00a.m. -6.00p.m. Admission 20p for children, 30p for adults, unless you happen to be an ex-Service man in uniform, when it is free.

This is the largest and most powerful cruiser ever built for the Royal Navy and the last surviving big-gun ship now housing a permanent Royal Navy Museum. There are guns galore, the bridge to command her from, and a film of the preparation for and the actual *D-Day Landings*, to give you some idea of what it was like to be in action. Perhaps you could combine a visit to the ship with a boat trip from Charing Cross and a visit to the Tower.

The Cutty Sark moored at Greenwich Pier SE10. 01-858-3445

Rail: British Rail to Greenwich. Open weekdays 11.00-5.00p.m., Sundays 2.30-5.00p.m. Admission children 5p, adults 10p.

A beautiful ship and the last of the great sailing clippers which used to race home round the Horn with their cargoes of tea, the Cutty Sark is now in dry dock as an educational centre for the Merchant Marine and as a museum. She is a very romantic ship crammed with fascinating maritime relics with a collection of super figureheads.

Gipsy Moth IV moored at Greenwich Pier SE10. 01-858-0245

Open weekdays 11.00-6.00p.m. Sundays 2.30-6.00 p.m. Admission children 3p, adults 8p.

You can go aboard Sir Francis Chichester's brave little boat in which he sailed alone around the world, to examine the equipment and wonder how on earth he managed it.

RIVER TRIPS

During the summer from about Easter until October, there are many boats to join for a trip on the river. They leave for the Tower and Greenwich from Westminster and Charing Cross piers approximately every hour. From Westminster pier boats leave for Hampton Court every half hour until noon, then every half hour for Putney, Kew and Richmond only. You can also go on a special boat from Westminster to the Battersea Fun Fair. Some of these boats are very grand, with bars and refreshments and shelter from the rain. Some have guides to point out the things you shouldn't miss along the way. Others are small, and have little but an inadequate awning to protect you should it rain. So take your choice, but it is wise to be prepared for the worst and take a warm sweater and a mac, as it is always colder on the river than on land. Binoculars are a good extra and add to the fun. It is advisable to telephone to check times of departure and cost of the trip. The number for the Thames Passenger Launch Service is 01-930-2074.

Another excursion which should be great fun if the difficulties arising from the driftwood which chokes the river can be overcome is by *Hydrofoil.* The Thames Arrow Express Company, 52 Fetter Lane,

EC4, 01-858-9712, hopes to run trips from Greenwich to Westminster, the Tower and maybe even to Woolwich or Gravesend. You will have to write or telephone to discover whether they are in operation or not.

To Greenwich

From Westminster or Charing Cross, or Tower Pier, the journey should take about 45 minutes. You can do the round trip, but you may want to return by land, which is easiest from Greenwich by British Rail to Charing Cross.

The river trip is definitely a grandstand view of London for the river winds its way past so much of London's past and present. From your vantage point on board you get great views of County Hall and the huge (and some say ugly) Shell Building, towering over the Royal Festival Hall. Almost opposite is the Savoy Hotel built on the site of a medieval palace. You pass the Mermaid Theatre and Billingsgate Fish Market, and maybe smell the latter too. St. Paul's great dome towers above the skyline, then on past the Tower and the now bricked up Traitor's Gate, under Tower Bridge and into what used to be the start of the docks.

Until 1800 shipping moored in the river was an easy target for pirates who used to cut the boats adrift and raid their holds when they drifted ashore. Gangs known as the River Pirates, the Light and Heavy Horsemen, and the Mudlarks were notorious and stole such quantities of cargo that the huge St. Katherine and London Docks were built to give protection against them. Now they stand empty, awaiting re-development, though some are used as studios, while the business of the port is carried on further downstream. You can still see that favourite haunt of smugglers, the pub called *The Prospect of Whitby*. The boat chugs on round the great loop of the river, Limehouse Reach and the Isle of Dogs, to the Royal Navy Victualling Yards. These have been royal docks from Henry VIII's time and many ships that sailed to defeat the Armada were built here. It was here too, aboard the *Golden Hind,* that Elizabeth I knighted Sir Francis Drake. A little way ahead you see the hill of Greenwich Park forming a background to one of the most exciting views in London.

The Royal Naval College, Greenwich SE20.

Open daily except Thursdays 2.30 - 5.00p.m.

This is the site of the favourite Palace of King Henry VII and of his son King Henry VIII, who was born here, as were his two daughters, Queen Mary and Queen Elizabeth I. During Cromwell's Commonwealth his men stripped the palace of its furniture and turned it into a biscuit factory, which can't have improved its already rather dilapidated state. The present building was begun as a palace for Charles II and continued by Sir Christopher Wren as a Naval Hospital. You can visit the Chapel and the amazing Painted Hall. The beautiful walls and ceiling are the work of Sir Thomas Thornhill.

National Maritime Museum and Queen's House, Greenwich SE10. 01-858-4422.

Open weekdays 10.00a.m.-5.00p.m. Saturdays 10.00-6.00p.m. Sundays 2.30-6.00p.m.

Queen's House, a marvellous building by Inigo Jones, is part of the museum which concentrates on Naval History from the time of the Tudors to the present day. Portraits of all the famous naval commanders stare haughtily from the walls alongside models of ships, uniforms and figureheads. Nelson is granted a room to himself for a collection of his belongings and memorabilia. There is a case full of carvings made by French prisoners of war to while away the time during which they were kept in the great prison hulks during the Napoleonic Wars.

Old Royal Observatory, Flamstead House, Greenwich, SE10. 01-858-4422.

Open weekdays 10.00a.m.-6.00p.m. Sundays 2.30-6.00p.m.

Designed by Wren, this was the original observatory of the first Astronomer Royal, Flamstead. It contains instruments of astronomical and navigational interest and is world famous for the zero meridian of longitude which passes through it and is marked on the path to the north of the building. Greenwich Mean Time is still our Standard Time.

Greenwich Tunnel

Built in 1902 to be a pedestrian tunnel linking Greenwich to the Isle of Dogs, the entrance to the footway is in Cutty Sark Gardens. Marvellously eerie to feel you are underneath all that water, plus a magnificent view of the Greenwich buildings from the gardens on the other side, where there are playgrounds and refreshment rooms.

Greenwich Park

Climb the hill behind the museum to the statue of General Sir John Wolfe, and enjoy one of the best views of the river and the East End of London This is a great place for a picnic.

Trip to Putney, Kew, Richmond, or Hampton Court

Boats leave Westminster Pier half-hourly throughout the day, but you must catch one before noon if you wish to go all the way to Hampton Court as it takes 3½ hours. It may not be a good idea to take very young children who cannot stand sitting still for any length of time. You can return by land, either to

Waterloo by British Rail from any of the stops, by tube from Putney Bridge, Kew and Richmond, or Green Line Bus 716 or 718 from Hampton Court to Hyde Park Corner. This journey will take you from the heart of London, where Big Ben sounds the hour high above the Houses of Parliament, right into the green of the country. It must have been quite a haul for the Royal Watermen as they rowed the huge State Barge upstream to Henry VIII's other favourite river palace, even with the tide to help.

As the riverboat chugs by the Tate Gallery, imagine the vast prison which once stood on the marshes of Millbank, and then look across to the other bank where the cranes are now busy building the new vegetable market to replace Covent Garden. The great hulk of Battersea Power Station with its four chimneys looking like some huge up-turned table, towers above the park and Battersea Fun Fair, whilst the boat continues upstream under Albert's suspension bridge. This bears a polite notice requesting troops to break step as they cross it, for otherwise the road begins to bounce alarmingly. Houseboats huddle in the shadow of Battersea Bridge and the warehouses and factories of industrial Fulham and Wandsworth give the river a very workworn appearance, until it reaches the boathouse-lined embankment of Putney. Here people are busy following the Water Rat's example, and are "simply messing about in boats". Eights carve up the water, their blades dipping to the shrill timekeeping of their cox, or obey the shouts from their coach as he braves a furious dash along the towpath, controlling bike and megaphone at once. Single lonely scullers, like insect waterboatmen, glance apprehensively over their shoulders in case some driftwood or a careless motorboat should barge into them. Dinghies tack back and forth occasionally capsizing, to the delight of onlookers, and the roar of a motorboat competes with the roar of the crowd across the river at Fulham Football ground. From Putney you follow the Boat Race Course, all four exhausting miles and 374 yards to the finish at Mortlake, passing Harrods Depository, Hammersmith Bridge, Chiswick Eyot, Barnes and the Brewery, all made famous by BBC commentators. Next comes the countryside of Kew Gardens and the Capability Brown landscape of Syon House opposite; then round the next bend to the lovely town of Richmond. The tidal reach of the Thames ends at Teddington Lock, and you have only to pass Kingston before you arrive at Hampton Court.

Hampton Court Palace, East Molesey, Surrey. 01-977-8441.

British Rail from Waterloo to Hampton Court station. Green Line Bus 716/718. Open: May to September 9.30 a.m.-6.00p.m. Sundays 11.00a.m.-4.45p.m. November to February 9.30a.m.-3.45p.m. Sundays 2.00-3.45p.m. March, April & October 9.30a.m.-4.45p.m. Sundays 2.00-4.45p.m. Closed Good Friday, Christmas Eve and Day, Boxing Day. Admission - Children & OAP 5p, Adults 20p except in October to March when adults are only 10p because Banqueting House, Great Kitchen Cellars & Tudor Tennis Court closed.

The Palace was built for Cardinal Wolsey in 1515 but he tactfully gave it to Henry VIII who was jealous of its splendours, to which he later added. It is said to be haunted by two of his unhappy wives, Jane Seymour who died here after giving birth to Edward VI, and his fifth wife, Catherine Howard, who was beheaded. Wren added the east and west wings to the original Tudor brick building. The house is full of superb pictures, furniture and tapestries. The Great Kitchen and Cellars, and the Tudor Tennis Court where Henry so enjoyed his game of Real Tennis are all fascinating, but you may be most intrigued by the famous Maze. The gardens are open all year round and have very romantic names: the Elizabethan Knott

Garden, the Great Fountain Garden, and the King's Privy Garden. Try to decipher the astronomical clock which tells not only the times of the tides, but the day, month, year and the phases of the moon.

RACES ON THE RIVER

The University Boat Race

Tube: Putney Bridge for the start of the course. British Rail to Mortlake for the finish, Hammersmith Broadway for half-way.

Raced annually on a Saturday at the end of March or beginning of April between the eights representing Oxford and Cambridge, the course is 4 miles 374 yds. long, from Putney Bridge to Mortlake. The two boats are followed by dozens of launches carrying judges and supporters which almost create a tidal wave in their wake. Watch from the towpath, from bridges or from Hammersmith and Chiswick Mall. Often one boat seems to get far ahead early on, but if the crews are evenly matched it can develop into an exciting battle.

The Head of the River Race

Rowed over the same course, this event takes place on a Saturday just before the Boat Race, but you have 300 crews and 3,000 competitors to watch. It is a thrilling sight and the noise is deafening.

Doggett's Coat and Badge

A very old (1716) race and a very tough one, rowed between the professional watermen who compete against the tide for a prize of £10 and the orange livery coat and badge presented by the Fishmongers' Company. The members of the Company turn up in splendid rig to watch the race from the Old Swan Pier, London Bridge to the Cadogan Pier in Chelsea.

Watch from Victoria Embankment, the bridges or Chelsea Embankment.

Swan-Upping

Not a race, but quite a sight as the swans vigorously resist attempts by six boatloads of officials to count and mark them. The swans on the Thames are owned by the Queen and by the Vintners' and Dyers' Companies. Once a year the birds are rounded up to be counted and the clear-billed birds which have reached maturity are marked. The marking or "upping" is made by cutting the upper mandible of the bird and stopping the slight bleeding with pitch. Birds with two marks on either side of the beak belong to the Vintners and those with one mark on the right side belong to the Dyers. The Queen's birds are no longer marked and number about 500, compared to the 65 owned by the Dyers, and 45 by the Vintners. Swan-upping takes place during July or August. Details from the Vintners' Swan Master, 01-546-2434, or the Dyers' Swan Keeper, 01-788-5643.

Towpaths

You can walk for miles along the river on the towpaths. Occasionally you have to cross a bridge and continue on the other bank when the path suddenly stops. At low tide you can do a bit of beachcombing or try to identify the plants and trees which grow along the banks. The beaches are inclined to be slippery with fine mud, and are often smelly, so you will need gumboots and parental permission first. Start at Putney Bridge, past the boathouses and playground and along the south bank beside playing fields and reservoirs to the suspension bridge at Hammersmith. Cross the bridge and continue along the north bank through the villages of Hammersmith and Chiswick, along Lower Mall and through gardens laid over a bombsite to the old riverside pub, *The Dove*. Then along Upper Mall, Hammersmith Terrace and Chiswick Mall where there are some lovely houses. There is a sailing club where you can watch the members at work, and lots of places to sit and watch the river flow by. Opposite the island known as Chiswick Eyot, the tide sweeps over the road, leaving driftwood in heaps. We used to collect it, dry it and use it for firewood when we lived here. At the far end of the Mall is St. Nicholas'Church, which, with the Chiswick Cemetery behind it, is a happy hunting ground for monuments and gravestones. Alongside it is Powell's Walk, an alley between high walls, which leads to Burlington Avenue and the Chertsey Road, and so to Chiswick House. The grounds are marvellous to play in with huge cedar trees whose branches sweep the ground; thickets of rhododendron; statues of sphinxes and lions, (which everyone rides though we suspect this is not really allowed). There is a lake fringed with duck to feed and to watch on their nests; and a sweeping double staircase to race up to the entrance of the house. Built to Lord Burlington's own plans, it is a perfect miniature Palladian villa, a party house and a home for his library. Built in 1765 it was damaged by a bomb during the war, but it has been beautifully restored. To join the river again you must follow the Chertsey road to Chiswick Bridge. The Brewery at Mortlake often smells strongly of hops and the sewage works a little further along the bank worse. But this is definitely one of the finest walks in London, and you can continue all the way to Richmond via Kew Gardens, though the river loops about crazily, so it is a very long way. Look on the map before you decide whether small children can manage it.

SIGHT-SEEING

TRAVELLING

London Transport Travel Enquiry Offices (01-222-1234) will give you any information you need about travel on London's Red Buses or Underground system. You can get free Bus and Underground maps from any of the offices, which are at Victoria, Oxford Circus, Piccadilly Circus, St. James's Park, King's Cross and Euston. They will also provide you with their *"Day Out"* leaflets, which describe different areas of interest and give detailed travel instructions. They are open every day, including Sunday, from 8.30 a.m. to 9.30 p.m. It may be a cliché, but the best way to see London is still from the top of a bus. The maximum fare for a child after 9.30a.m. is 3p. For adults the maximum fare is 12p at *off peak travel* times; 9.30 a.m.-4.00 p.m., 7.00 p.m.-12.30 a.m. Mondays to Fridays, Saturdays, Sundays and Public Holidays 4.30 p.m. till 12.30 a.m. London Transport run a very good two hour *Round London Sightseeing Tour* which takes in most of the famous landmarks. During the evening many of the buildings are floodlit. They run every day, except on Christmas Day, from Piccadilly Circus from 10.00a.m. to 9.00 p.m. and from Victoria from 10.00a.m. to 4.00 p.m. Children 45p, adults 65p. If you plan to go far a *Red Bus Rover* ticket will save you money. It covers a day's unlimited travel on red buses on the 1,500 miles and 300 routes run by London Transport, for 25p if you are under 14, 50p otherwise. They are valid after 9.30 a.m. on Mondays to Fridays and obtainable at all London Transport Enquiry Offices, some Underground stations or from bus garages; they *cannot* be bought from the conductor. Buy them on the day or up to seven days in advance. See how far you can go in a day, or how many statues you can find or play Scavenger with places to collect instead of things. If you are really bent on serious sightseeing over four days or a week, you would do well to buy a *Tourist Ticket,* which gives you unlimited travel on all *red buses* and over the whole Underground system as well. Each ticket entitles you to a free ride on the *Round London Sightseeing Tour* as well. They cost £1.30 (£2.90 adult) for four days, £1.50 (£3.80 adult) for seven days, and are obtainable at all London Transport Enquiry Offices, together with a Tourist Information Folder.

Another season ticket which will save you money is one which will admit you to all the historic monuments in the care of the State. They cost 37½p (75p for adults) for a year, and are obtainable from *The Secretary (AMSS/P), Department of the Environment, Room 204, Neville House, Page Street, SW1.* In London the monuments concerned are the Banqueting House in Whitehall, Chiswick House, Eltham Palace, Greenwich Royal Naval College, Chapel and the Painted Hall, Hampton Court Palace, the Jewel Tower at Westminster, Kew Palace, King Henry VIII's Wine Cellar, Lancaster House, London Wall, the Queen's Cottage at Kew, The Tower and Crown Jewels, Westminster Abbey Chapter House and Pyx Chamber.

To find out what events are taking place in London you can dial 01-246-8041, or 01-246-8007 for Ed. Stewart (Stewpot's) version for children. For further information contact the *London Tourist Board, 4*

Grosvenor Gardens, SW1 (01-730-0791) or for personal callers only, the *British Tourist Authority, 64
St. James's Street, SW1.*

*The City of London Information Service, St. Paul's
Churchyard, EC4 (01-606-3030)* will help you too.
Should you come up against a blank, the *Daily Tele-
graph Information Bureau (01-353-4242)* will give
you information on almost any subject. If you lose
something, contact the *Lost Property Office, 200
Baker Street, W1.* Go there between 10.00 a.m.-
6.00 p.m. Monday to Friday (closed on Public Holidays) or contact your nearest police station. If you
get lost yourself, go straight to the nearest policeman
and explain. He will see that you get home safely.

For information about any of the GLC Parks, contact the *Parks Dept., Cavell House, 2a Charing Cross
Road, London, WC2H 0HJ (01-836-5464).*

THE CITY

The City must be thick with ghosts. People have
lived here since the Stone Age. The Romans established
a major settlement which was attacked and burnt to
the ground by Boudicca (Boadicea) and her people of
the Iceni. It has been a "celebrated centre of com-
merce" since Tacitus so described it in AD 60. When
you remember that the City has seen Kings crowned,
Queens beheaded, has been the scene of riot, plague
and fire, and has survived the bombs that rained down
on it only thirty years ago, it all looks rather tame and
boring with its drab office blocks and business men
in bowlers. But you can discover proof of its past if
you do some detective work, and there is no better
place to start than at the Tower of London.

Tower of London, Tower Hill, EC3 (01-709-0765)

Open from March to October, Mondays to Saturdays 9.30 a.m.-5.30 p.m. Sundays 2.00 p.m.- 5.00 p.m. November to February Mondays to Saturdays only 9.30 a.m.-4.00 p.m. Closed Good Fridays, Christmas and Boxing Days. Admission Children 5p, adults 20p. Admission to the Jewel House Children 5p, adults 10p. Unaccompanied children under ten not admitted. Written application to the Governor for tickets to the Ceremony of the Keys. Tube: Tower Hill.

William the Conqueror built the White Tower in 1078 to impress and frighten his new subjects, since when it has been fortress, royal palace, prison above all else, and is still an arsenal with a garrison. It has a history of violence to which the instruments of torture in the Crypt of the Chapel of St. John bear witness. Sir Thomas More, Elizabeth I and Monmouth were among the prisoners held in the Bell Tower. The little princes Edward V and the Duke of York were murdered in the Bloody Tower and Anne Boleyn and Catherine Howard died on the block at Tower Green. You can visualize Henry VIII who so mercilessly sent them there when you see his two sets of armour in the museum of the White Tower. One was made for the slim Hal, the other for the Henry who was "fat as a pig" and is as vast as he was, measuring 52 inches around. There is armour for a real elephant too and for the horses which had to carry their masters into battle. In a vault below the Waterloo Barracks the Crown Jewels are dazzling in their burglar-proof cases with two of the world's biggest diamonds, the Koh-i-noor and all 530 carats of the Star of India. The coronation insignia dates from the time of Charles II because Cromwell's government had melted down the originals (There is often a long queue to see the Jewels, so be prepared). Outside the massive stone walls of the White Tower the ravens are cared for by the Yeoman Warders. Legend has it that the Tower will fall if ever the ravens leave it, so they are rather specially cossetted. One of the best times to see the Tower is at night when it is floodlit, and if you are allowed to stay up late, try to see the Ceremony of the Keys. This takes place every night about 10.00 p.m. as the Guard locks the Tower against the enemies of Her Majesty. Outside the Tower is the great wide expanse of the Thames, overlooked by the cannon which are fired by the Honourable Artillery Company on occasions such as the anniversary of the Queen's accession. You may be lucky and see Tower Bridge in action, the road can be lifted in 90 seconds to allow shipping to pass underneath. The machinery which has worked so efficiently for so long is being replaced and there are plans to open the walkway to the public, but they have yet to be decided.

Back on Tower Hill you will discover more of London's hidden history in the crypt of the Church of All Hallows Barking, where you will find Saxon and Roman relics. The great "lion heart" of Richard I is said to be buried here too. On the east side of Trinity Square you can see a fragment 50 ft long of what remains of the original Roman Wall, and in the middle of the Square the bloodthirsty site of countless be-headings marked by a rectangle of paving with chains around it, the old scaffold of Tower Hill.

The Monument, Fish Street Hill, EC4

Mondays to Saturdays 9.00 a.m.-6.00 p.m. (4.00 p.m. in winter). Sundays open May-September from 2.00-6.00 p.m. Admission children 2½p, adults 5p. Tube: Monument.

Climb the 311 steps of the Monument for a fabulous but very out-of-breath view of the City and imagine how things must have looked during the Great Fire of 1666 which it commemorates. Designed by Wren, it is 202 ft high and 202 ft from the spot in nearby Pudding Lane where the fire broke out to rage through the close-packed wooden houses, destroying 13,000 of them, 89 churches and 436 acres of London as it went. The ash fell as far away as Eton. Round the base of the column is a relief showing London destroyed and London restored. The splendid gentleman so curiously dressed in a wig and a Roman kilt is Charles II who is encouraging Time in his work of restoration. Monument has its own tube station, and from here you can ride on an escalator all the way to the Bank.

Bank

This is a junction of seven streets and the hub of the City. The three great buildings you can see as you emerge from below represent the three aspects of the City. The Bank of England itself, the "old Lady of Threadneedle Street", with our gold reserve in solid gold ingots stored in the vaults, represents money. The Royal Exchange represents trade as its name implies, and the Mansion House, which is the home of the Lord Mayor of London, stands for the Corporation and for the City's independence. (The City has its own special policemen, the City of London Police who wear crested helmets and red and white armbands to distinguish them from the Metropolitan Police). All around you are banks and insurance and city companies. The poulterers and the corn market which the street names suggest have long since disappeared. Where our business men worship Mammon the Romans once honoured the Sun God, Mithras. You will find the foundations of the Temple to Mithras in Temple Court, Queen Victoria Street, EC4. You will have to visit the Guildhall Museum (see Museums) to see the things that were discovered here during the excavations.

St. Pauls Cathedral, Ludgate Hill, EC4 (01-236-4128)

Tube: St Pauls. Mondays to Saturdays 11.00 a.m.-3.30 p.m. In summer from 4.45 p.m. or 5.30 p.m. The

Chancel and Nave have free admission, Galleries 15p, and 20p, Crypt 10p and 15p.

Choose a clear day and feel even stronger than you did for your assent of the Monument for this time you have 627 steps ahead of you as you climb to the top. Up through the Whispering Gallery where your secrets can be heard on the other side of the dome, past the Stone Gallery and on up into the Golden Ball above the Golden Gallery. The cross above you is 365 ft from the ground, and you have the most fantastic view of the City, a panorama of spires and towers, laid out before you. See whether you can spot some of Wren's other churches, he was responsible for 50 apart from his great masterpiece, the Cathedral itself. The great bell of one of them, St Mary-le-Bow, (a reconstruction, the original was destroyed in the Blitz) called Dick Whittington back to be Lord Mayor of London four times. If you remember your nursery rhymes and have a map you may be able to make out the whereabouts of all the bells of Oranges and Lemons. Below you is Cheapside (cheap from the old English 'cyppan' which means to bargain) and many streets whose names tell you their original function, Bread Street, Milk and Wood Street, Ironmonger Lane. The merchants and people who thronged the streets often used the old Gothic Cathedral, destroyed in the Fire, as an extension to the market, and in 1385 the church authorities had to ban ball playing in the nave. It was even worse later when Cromwell used it as a barracks for his cavalrymen and their horses.

The present Cathedral is the largest and perhaps the most famous in the world. It was designed by Sir Christopher Wren whose epitaph is in the crypt, "Si Monumentum requiris circumspice" (if you seek a memorial look about you). It took him and his team of master builders and craftsmen 35 years to finish. The choir stalls and organ case are carved by the genius Grinling Gibbons. The ironwork is by the famous

Frenchman, Tijou. The church is magnificent under its great Dome, which is the largest in the world after St. Peter's in Rome, and peopled with marble statues of the nation's heroes. For the best monuments you must visit the Crypt, huge and dark and errie under its massive arches. Here is Painter's Corner with memorials to artists, and here you will find Wellington's funeral carriage and his grave. Nelson is buried nearby in a beautiful black marble tomb. Some of the remains of monuments from the old St Paul's which were recovered after the Great Fire are stored in the west end of the Crypt.

Trafalgar Square, Whitehall and Westminster Abbey

Try to arrive in Trafalgar Square just before 10.00 a.m. when the fountains suddenly explode into life with jets of water, which the wind snatches and turns to a fine spray. Climb to the balcony of the National Gallery for the best view of Nelson in his cocked hat and with empty sleeve, 184 ft above the crooning pigeons waiting for you to feed them below. His column is guarded by Landseer's four magnificent lions and around its base are reliefs depicting his sea battles and his death in the arms of Hardy on board HMS Victory at Trafalgar in 1805. Two other interesting statues for you to add to your collection are the equestrian George IV bareback and barefoot and ludicrously dressed in a toga, and in equally odd costume of laurel wreath and Roman kilt, the Grinling Gibbon statue of James II. In the crypt of St. Martins-in-the-Fields you can see monuments from the old church, an eighteenth century whipping post, and Gibb's model for the present church. Charles II was christened here and his most famous girlfriend, Nell Gwynn, is buried here. Make your way through the cloud of pigeons, frantically feeding from outstretched hands, to the statue of the martyred King Charles I who appears to be going to join you on your way down

Whitehall. The statue was sold by Parliament to be melted down after his execution, but it was secretly buried and reinstated by royalists at his son's Restoration. Whitehall has been thick with civil servants ever since Henry VIII made the Palace of Whitehall his main London palace and moved the government's administration to join him, although Parliament remained at Westminster. The Palace was burnt to the ground in 1698 and nothing remains but the beautiful Banqueting House (open Tuesdays to Saturdays 10.00 a.m.-5.00 p.m., Sundays 2.00-5.00 p.m.) built in 1619 by Inigo Jones. You must look at the ceiling painted by Rubens to the glorification of the House of Stuart. It was on a scaffold outside that the most unfortunate Stuart of all was beheaded in 1649. The Banqueting House is half-way down Whitehall, so first you must pass the Admiralty, and its two beautiful seahorses as you go to watch the Changing of the Guard at Horseguards. This takes place at 11.00 a.m. every morning, with a great clashing of bands and tramping of boots. The crowds are thick so try to get a good place by arriving early. If you miss it, look at the patient troopers of the Household Cavalry, motionless on their well-behaved horses in their twin sentry boxes. The Life Guards wear red tunics with white plumes, the Royal and Blues wear blue tunics with red plumes. Further down the road turn up Downing Street, where you must persuade someone to take your photograph on the steps of No. 10, in case you ever become Prime Minister, as Harold Wilson did. You may see someone important arriving, perhaps the Cabinet for a meeting, or the Chancellor of the Exchequer returning to his home next door at No. 11. Back in Whitehall and in the middle of the road, the Cenotaph, bright with flags and poppies, in memory of the dead of two World Wars. The Foreign Office and the Treasury are just two of the many Government offices which line the road.

Parliament Square, at the bottom of Whitehall, is

full of statues of various statesmen. We always longed to ask Lincoln to sit down on the empty chair behind him, and Smuts leans forward at such an uncomfortable angle. In St Margaret's the parish church of the House of Commons, you can see a magnificent stained glass window which dates from 1501 and was made on on the occasion of Catherine of Aragon's betrothal to Prince Arthur. Around the corner, set in a little moat with goldfish gleaming in the water, is the Jewel Tower, the only remaining part of the old Palace of Westminster, and originally Edward III's private treasury. It is now a museum of relics of the Palace and documents concerning it. Open weekdays 10.30 a.m.-6.30 p.m. From October till February it closes at 4.00 p.m.

Westminster Abbey off Parliament Square, SW1 (01-222-1051)

Open daily but there are services at 9.20 a.m. and 5.00 p.m. so avoid these times. Admission to Royal Chapels, children 5p, adults 15p. Museum, children 5p. and adults 10p. Tube: Westminster

This great Gothic church was founded by Edward the Confessor in 1050, since when it has been the scene of the coronations of all our sovereigns from William the Conqueror to Elizabeth II, except for two Edwards, the V and VIII. It is a superb place and Henry VII's chapel the most exquisite example of Gothic architecture with its amazing fan-vault ceiling. The church contains the Grave of the Unknown Warrior, and hundreds of graves and monuments to the famous men and women of British history, with Kings, Queens, princes and princesses (the two saddest the tiny infant daughters of James I, Sophia aged 3 days, and Mary aged 2 years). Poet's Corner remembers Chaucer, Spenser, Ben Johnson and Milton amongst many others. Behind the High Altar is the Coronation Chair which enclosed the Stone of Scone, which

26

Edward I brought back from Scotland, and which is occasionally stolen back again. In the Museum there is an extraordinary collection of effigies with wax faces and wooden bodies clad in the clothes of those they represent. Nelson is amongst them, and you can see his famous cocked hat, and his green eyepatch too.

Houses of Parliament, Westminster, SW1 (01-219-3000)

Tube: Westminster. Saturdays 10.00 a.m.-5.00 p.m. Also Easter Monday and Tuesday; Mondays Tuesdays and Thursdays in August and Thursdays in September from 10.00 a.m.-5.00 p.m. The House of Commons sits from 2.30 p.m. Mondays-Thursdays and 11.30 a.m. on Fridays. The House of Lords sits from 2.30 p.m. on Tuesdays and Wednesdays and from 3.00 p.m. on Thursdays.

The Houses of Parliament stand on the site of the old Royal Palace of Westminster which replaced Winchester as the seat of government early in the eleventh century. It was to Westminster that Simon de Montfort summoned the shire representatives in 1265. Until 1530, when the Crown moved house up the road to Whitehall, it was a royal palace as well as the headquarters of the Church and Law. In 1834 the building was burnt to the ground and only Westminster Hall, the crypt of St Stephen's Chapel and the Jewel Tower survived. The present splendid Victorian Gothic building was designed by Sir Charles Barry and A.W.N. Pugin and completed in 1868. It contains 1,100 apartments, 100 staircases, 11 courtyards, and two miles of passage. The Victoria Tower is the tallest of the two towers, 336 ft high in comparison to the 320 ft of the Clock Tower which everyone knows as Big Ben. Big Ben in fact is the name of the famous bell which sounds the hour. It weighs 13½ stone and was called after Sir Benjamin Hall who was the Commissioner of Works when the bell was hung. The minute hand of the clock is 14 ft long. During the day the Union

Jack flies from the top of the Victoria Tower when the House is sitting, and at night, until the House rises, a light shines from the top of the Clock Tower. You can tour the Houses of Parliament on Saturdays and on some days during Recess, when the Members of Parliament are on holiday. You enter the Victoria Tower and climb the Royal Staircase to the Robing Room, which is the route the Queen takes when she arrives to open Parliament. Paintings of the legend of King Arthur decorate the walls and in the Royal Gallery next door you can see two magnificent paintings - one of the Death of Nelson, the other of Wellington meeting Blucher. Then into the House of Lords, where the Peers of the Realm conduct their business. The Lord Chancellor presides from his seat, just below the Royal Throne, on the Woolsack, a reminder of the days when Britain's wealth depended on the wool trade. At the far end of the room is the Bar, which is where the Commons, led by the Speaker, attend the Opening of Parliament. The Sovereign has not been allowed into the House of Commons since the day when Charles I stormed in to demand the arrest of five members. From the Peer's Lobby, which is decorated with the arms of the six dynasties of the Kings of England (Saxon, Norman, Plantagenet, Tudor, Stuart and Hanoverian) you go by way of the Peer's Corridor to the Central Lobby. This is where you can come to 'lobby' your MP. The House of Commons was destroyed by a bomb in 1941, and stones, damaged by the fire, were used to build the Churchill Arch which leads into it. The Government and Opposition sit facing each other, the Cabinet and Shadow Cabinet on the front benches which are still divided by two red lines exactly two swords' length apart! Each day's session is opened by a procession led by the Speaker impressive in black knee-breeches, gown and wig, and attended by the Sergeant-at-Arms carrying the Mace, his train-bearer, chaplain and secretary. You can listen to the debates from the Strangers' Gallery. You must write to your MP asking him to reserve you a seat if you wish to be sure of getting in when the House opens at 2.30 p.m. for Question Time. This is usually the most interesting time to attend. You do not need a ticket after Question Time ends at 4.00 p.m., but you have to queue at St Stephen's Hall. You can listen in on the House of Lords too. You do not need a ticket but should join the queue about an hour before the House opens.

Westminster Hall is the oldest surviving part of the Old Palace, originally built by William Rufus in 1097 but remodelled for Richard II between 1394-1402 by the greatest architect of English Gothic, Yevele. This was when the magnificent oak hammer-beam roof was constructed. From the 13th Century to the 19th this was the chief law court of England. Richard II was deposed here, Sir Thomas More was sentenced to death here, and Charles I stood trial for his life here. In the Central Lobby is a statue of the man who was instrumental in bringing him to the scaffold, that great Parliamentarian, Oliver Cromwell. He is commemorated twice, warts and all, with another statue outside the Hall. There are other interesting statues too. Richard, Coeur de Lion, rides through Old Palace Yard, the site of the scaffold where Sir Walter Raleigh died and where Guy Fawkes and some of his Gunpowder Plot Colleagues were executed after their unsuccessful attempt to blow the whole place sky high. In Victoria Tower Gardens is the Rodin statue of the Burghers of Calais, who so bravely surrendered themselves to Edward III to save their town. Nearby is the great suffragette leader, Mrs. Pankhurst, and Women's Lib supporters amongst you might like to find another heroine, as she calmly controls her chariot above the swirling traffic at the approach to Westminster Bridge. This is Boudicca (or Boadicea) on her way to attack the Romans at Londinium perhaps.

MUSEUMS

There are so many museums and galleries in London that even if it rained on every Sunday of the year, there would still not be time to discover all their treasures. Marvellous days can be spent browsing round them and finding all sorts and conditions of interesting, weird and wonderful things. There are beautiful and precious things; things scientific; engines and embroidery; paintings and pistols; things from pre-history to tomorrow's inventions; things you can understand and things incomprehensible; there they all are, waiting. Most museums are free, some charge a small entrance fee and some charge for special exhibitions. Many of them have activities planned for children on Saturdays and during the school holidays, with art rooms, lectures, films and quizzes. Some museums are so huge that it is only possible to give you a general idea of their contents, and to pick out some of the most fascinating. We have given details of opening times and telephone numbers, so that you can check up on special activities and exhibitions.

THREE FOR STARTERS

British Museum, Great Russell Street WC1 (01-636 1555)

Tubes: Tottenham Court Road, Goodge Street, Russell Square, Holborn. Open weekdays 10.00a.m.-5.00 p.m. Sundays 2.30-6.00 p.m. Closed Good Friday, Christmas Eve and Day, Boxing Day. Refreshment room.

The world's largest, this museum contains a staggering collection of treasures historical, archaeological and artistic. It is also the National Library which, because it holds a compulsory copyright deposit, has a copy of every book printed in Britain since 1911, and a storage problem to match. You can look into the huge Reading Room where writers are busy on yet more books to join the millions, or search the museum for the most beautiful book ever produced - the illuminated Lindisfarne Gospels. It becomes difficult to decide what to concentrate on when you have the Elgin Marbles from the Parthenon, Greek and Roman sculpture, coins and medals, the Magna Carta and the famous Egyptian mummies to choose from. Compare African and Aztec art, or imagine the excitement when they discovered the Saxon treasures buried with a chieftain's ship at Sutton Hoo.

The Victoria & Albert Museum, South Kensington SW7 (01-589-6371)

Tube: South Kensington. Subway from station to museum entrance. Open weekdays 10.00 a.m.-6.00 p.m. Sundays 2.30-6.30 p.m. Closed Good Friday, Christmas Eve, Day, Boxing Day. Charge for special exhibitions. Restaurant and cafeteria.

You are bound to lose your way as you explore this enormous museum but there are many guides to direct you. They are especially helpful to children, giving encouragement to draw what you will, and sometimes providing stools to sit on. Here, going round the national collection of "Fine and Applied Art" you can examine all that is best in furniture, costumes, jewellery, porcelain, clocks, armour, embroideries, silver and jewellery in an impressive new gallery. Room upon room of fantastic things with art and antiquities from India and China, the Raphael cartoons, and portrait miniatures by Holbein and Hilliard. During the holidays there are sometimes lectures and film shows for children, or special exhibitions.

The Horniman Museum, London Road, Forest Hill SE23 (01-699-2339)

British Rail train to Forest Hill. Open weekdays 10.00 a.m.-6.00 p.m. Sundays 2.00-6.00 p.m. No children under 8 admitted, unless accompanied by a child of 13 and over, or an adult. Closed Christmas Eve and Christmas Day. Tea room.

Man and his Environment is the theme for this museum which has an extraordinary collection of objects illustrating man's religions and ways of life, as well as his progress from prehistoric times in the arts and crafts. There are examples of African, Ancient Egyptian, American Indian and Eskimo art, and a section devoted to musical instruments. An extensive Natural History collection includes animals from every continent, evolutionary exhibits, fossils and an Aquarium. Outside in the adjoining gardens are nature trails to follow. There is a Children's Centre for leisure activities, and a Club open to all children between 9 and 16 who are able to visit the museum fairly regularly, and who enjoy learning about things in the museum and using ideas from them in drawing, painting and craft work. Activities include modelling, pottery, toymaking, embroidery and lino block printing. Non-members are welcome to borrow drawing materials.

FOR MILITARY ENTHUSIASTS AND ARMOUR ADDICTS

Imperial War Museum, Lambeth Road SE1 (01-735 8922)

Tube: Lambeth North, Elephant and Castle. Weekdays 10.00 a.m.-6.00 p.m. Sunday 2.00-6.00 p.m. Closed Good Friday, Christmas Eve and Day, Boxing Day.

An enthralling collection of relics and records of both the World Wars, appropriately housed in what used to be Bethlehem Hospital (Bedlam), with two vast naval guns from HMS Ramillies and Resolution guarding the entrance. All the machinery of war; weapons, uniforms, equipment, and paintings by war artists bring the battle home. There are models of battlefields, naval engagements, field hospitals and a map to illustrate the background to the Great War. A claustrophobic one-man German submarine and a Spitfire from the 1940's contrasts with the old London bus used to carry troops to the Front line and the trenches of 1914.

National Army Museum, Royal Hospital Road, SW3 (01-730-0717)

Tube: Sloane Square, Car park. Weekdays 10.00 a.m. -5.30 p.m. Sundays and public holidays 2.00-5.30 p.m. Closed Good Friday, Christmas Eve and Day, Boxing Day.

London's newest museum concentrates on the history of the Army from the reign of Henry VII to 1914. You will be greeted in the hall by the skeleton of Napoleon's favourite horse, Marengo. Ask for the questionaire (1p) which will help you explore the splendid rooms full of uniforms and decorations, arms and armour, and find the diorama of the Zulus at the battle of Rorke's Drift. Music and soliders' songs appropriate to each period are on tape at the push of a button and some of the finest military pictures help to bring history to life.

Wellington Museum, Apsley House, Hyde Park Corner SW1. (01-499-3676)

Tube: Hyde Park Corner. Weekdays 10.00 a.m.-6.00 p.m. Sundays 2.30-6.00 p.m. Closed Good Friday Christmas Eve and Day, Boxing Day. Admission 5p for children, 10p for adults. Unaccompanied children under 14 not admitted.

Personal relics of the Duke of Wellington in his own house. Pictures and loot from his wars. (See Parks and Palaces).

Wallace Collection, Manchester Square W1.(01-935-1687)

Tube: Baker Street, Bond Street. Weekdays 10.00 a.m. -5.00 p.m. Sundays 2.00-5.00 p.m. Closed Good Friday, Christmas Eve and Christmas Day.

A super collection of arms and armour in a lovely 18th century house, with some of the most beautiful paintings in London as an added incentive. There are some very grand guns belonging to Captains and Kings, an absolutely stunning set of armour for man and horse, very Gothic and German, and some intriguing Indian armour too.

Artillery Museum, The Rotunda, Woolwich Common SE18 (01-854-2424)

Tube: New Cross. Weekdays 10.00 a.m.-12.45 p.m., 2.00-5.00 p.m. Saturdays 10.00 a.m.-12.00 p.m. Sundays 2.00-5.00 p.m. Closed Good Friday, Christmas Day. Unaccompanied children under 14 not admitted.

Closed until 1974 for repairs, but worth waiting for the array of guns, rockets, muskets, arms and armour.

SCIENCE SESSIONS

Science Museum, Exhibition Road, South Kensington SW7 (01-589-6371)

Tube: South Kensington, Subway from station to museum entrance. Weekdays 10.00 a.m.-6.00 p.m. Sundays 2.30-6.00 p.m. Closed Good Friday, Christmas Eve and Day, Boxing Day. Cafeteria.

Splendid museum for all age groups (not just boys either; the director is a woman) where the history and application of science are excitingly demonstrated, and many mysteries explained. There is a Children's Gallery where push-button addicts can have fun with the working models, and a section devoted to Transport where enthusiasts can indulge in model railways and engines, and examine the Caerphilly Castle, the Deltic, Rolls Royces, and a Mini cut away to show its works. From the oldest train in the world, the Puffing Billy of 1813, to the oldest aircraft, a model of the Wright brothers' aeroplane, which hangs amongst dozens of others, equally enthralling, in the giant hangar of the Aeronautics Gallery. Lectures during the holidays; special exhibitions.

Natural History Museum, Cromwell Road, South Kensington SW7. (01-589-6323)

Tube: South Kensington. Weekdays 10.00 a.m.-6.00 p.m. Sundays 2.30-6.00 p.m. Closed Good Friday, Christmas Eve and Day, Boxing Day. Cafeteria.

Chi-Chi the Giant Panda has now joined the hundreds of stuffed animals in this veritable Noah's Ark in South Kensington. Birdwatchers can study their feathered friends in close-up in the dioramas of birds in their natural habitat. Cases of jewel-bright butterflies and wicked looking spiders alongside others full of sponges, minerals, coral and fossils, provide wonderful subjects for sketching, and the Children's Centre will provide you with paper and pencil if you have forgotten your own. The most impressive room houses the dinosaurs, dwarfed by the 84 foot length of Diplodocus; but even more spectacular is the great Blue Whale, all 91 ft. of him, suspended above his lesser brethren in the Whale Room. Next door are shoals of fish. We used to guarantee peace for ourselves when young by betting little brothers they couldn't find the kipper; mean but effective.

Geological Museum, Exhibition Road, SW7. (01-589-5444)

Tube: South Kensington. Subway from station to museum entrance. Weekdays 10.00 a.m.-6.00 p.m. Sundays 2.30-6.00 p.m. Closed Good Friday, Christmas Eve and Day, Boxing Day.

A treasure trove of gemstones, replicas of world famous diamonds, opal, agate, lapis lazuli, amethyst, ruby, aquamarine, and dioramas illustrating the structure of the earth to help answer some of the more baffling geological questions. Examples of fossils, rocks and minerals fill in the picture. Frequent talks, demonstrations, films.

FOR HISTORICAL BACKGROUND, FURNITURE AND TOYS

Bethnal Green Museum, Cambridge Heath Road, E2 (01-980-3204)

Tube: Bethnal Green. Weekdays 10.00 a.m.-6.00 p.m. Sundays 2.30-6.00 p.m. Closed on public holidays.

A collection which features the history of the locality, and includes examples of silk woven at nearby Spitalfields, together with silver, pottery, paintings and costumes. There is also a delightful display of dolls and doll's houses. During the holidays there are special activities (send s.a.e. for details) and a workshop open to children on Saturdays from 11.00 a.m.-1.00 p.m., and from 2.00-4.00 p.m. with materials provided for drawing, painting, modelling in plasticine and weaving.

London Museum, Kensington Palace, W8 (01-937-9816)

Tube: Bayswater, Queensway, High Street Kensington. Weekdays 10.00 a.m.-6.00 p.m. Sundays 2.00-6.00 p.m. Closed Good Friday, Christmas Eve and Day, Boxing Day.

State Rooms of Palace open. In the museum is a collection of relics of London, from pre-history onwards. (See chapter on Palaces and Parks). Quiz paper and pencils at the door.

Pollock's Toy Museum, 1a Scala Street, W1.(01-636 -3452)

Tube: Tottenham Court Road, Goodge Street. Monday to Saturday 10.00 a.m.-5.00 p.m.

A tiny museum on three floors, it is also a shop, crammed to bursting with curious old dolls, toys and toy theatres. Demonstrations of Toy Theatres during term time on Thursdays and Saturdays, and Punch and Judy Shows are given during August (Telephone beforehand for exact times). Refreshments for sale include home-made gingerbread men.

Geffrye Museum, Kingsland Road, Shoreditch, E2 (01-739-8368)

Tube: Liverpool Street, Old Street. Bus: 22, 48, 67, 97, 149, 243. Tuesdays-Saturdays and Bank Holidays 10.00 a.m.-5.00 p.m. Sundays 2.00-5.00 p.m. Child-

rens' activities on Saturdays and school holidays
10.00-12.30 p.m. and 2.00-4.30 p.m. excluding Mondays and Sundays. Coffee Bar.

A very small and very friendly museum of furniture, the rooms are arranged in chronological order
from the time of Elizabeth I, with some shop fronts, a
woodworker's shop and an open-hearth kitchen for
good measure. There seem to be far more children
here than adults. One wing of this pretty group of
18th century Almshouses is devoted to a children's
room and art studio where you are welcome to paint,
draw or join groups for pottery, model-making, silk
screen painting or basketry on Saturdays and during
the school holidays. The staff are always ready to talk
and help you explore the museum, and there are
special worksheets to help you learn more about the
exhibits by drawing them, collecting information or
using puzzles. A very good place for getting the feel
of any period you may be studying.

**City of London Guildhall Museum, Gillette House,
55 Basinghall Street, EC2 (01-606-3030)**

*Tube: Bank, Moorgate. Monday-Saturday 10.00 a.m.-
5.00 p.m. Closed Good Friday, Easter Sunday and
Monday, Christmas Day, Boxing Day.*

London's past displayed in four galleries, one of
which houses an exhibition of leathercraft through
the ages and boasts a Roman bikini in leather. The
marble head of the Sun God is chief of the finds ex-
cavated at the Temple of Mithras and collected here.
There is also a reconstruction of life in Roman London,
which includes a Roman kitchen, and the third gallery
concentrates on relics of Medieval London. Especially
useful for school projects involving Romans.

FOR STAMP COLLECTORS

National Postal Museum, King Edward Building, King Edward Street, EC1. (01-432-3851)

Tube: St. Pauls. Monday-Friday 10.30 a.m.-4.30 p.m. Saturdays 10.00 a.m.-4.00 p.m. Closed Bank Holidays.

The Reginald M. Phillips Collection of stamps and the Post Office collection, includes priceless philatelic rarities, and is one of the most valuable collections in the world.

ART GALLERIES

The National Gallery, Trafalgar Square, WC2. (01-930-7618)

Tube: Trafalgar Square, Strand. Weekdays 10.00 a.m.-6.00 p.m. Sundays 2.00-6.00 p.m. Closed Christmas Eve and Day. Cafeteria.

Perhaps the finest collection of pictures in the world, this is guaranteed to give you mental indigestion if you try to see them all in one visit. Better to go and gaze at a few at a time; masterpieces from the 13th century to the early 20th century include Giotto, Peiro della Francesca, Raphael, Vermeer.

The National Portrait Gallery, St. Martin's Place, Trafalgar Square, WC2. (01-930-8511)

Tube: Trafalgar Square, Strand. Weekdays 10.00 a.m.-5.00 p.m. Sundays 2.00-6.00 p.m. Closed Good Friday, Christmas Eve and Day.

Search through this great collection of portraits of the famous and notable in Britain's history; check up on how your heroes looked. Some of the pictures are important works of art, others are only important because of the man or woman they portray. Henry VIII, Pepys, Nelson and Nell Gwynn rub shoulders with Jane Austen and Sir Christopher Wren. Holiday activities for children of 8-15, involving portraiture in some form or other. Send for details (sae).

Tate Gallery, Millbank, SW1. (01-828-4444)

Tube: Pimlico. Weekdays 10.00 a.m.-6.00 p.m. Sundays 2.00-6.00 p.m. Charge for special exhibitions. Restaurant.

The Tate houses the national collection of British painting from 1500 to the present day, as well as painting and sculpture of the modern Continental and American schools. Here you can compare the art of painters such as Reynolds, Gainsborough, Stubbs, Turner, Constable, Sargent and Sickert with their modern counterparts, and find out what you think of Cubism, Expressionism, Surrealism, Op and Pop Art.

Institute of Contemporary Arts, Nash House, The Mall SW1 (01-839-5344)

Tube: Trafalgar Square, Piccadilly. Tuesday-Saturday 12.00-8.00 p.m. Sundays 2.00-10.00 p.m. Closed Good Friday, Christmas Eve and Day, Boxing Day.

Frequently changing and exciting exhibitions of contemporary art, sometimes including things which demand involvement and co-operation, which is great fun. Films for children every Saturday and Sunday afternoon at 3.00 p.m. for 25p. Telephone for details.

PARKS AND PALACES

Exploring London on little money need not be difficult, in fact most of the best things to do and see are free. It is the getting there and the keeping going on ice-creams that run away with pocket money, so cut down on your travelling expenses by choosing to explore one district at a time and by taking a picnic and something to drink with you.

It is obvious that long days in the park will be most fun when the weather is warm, and that looking round museums will keep you dry when it is cold and wet, but in any case it is a good idea to combine the two. There is a limit to the amount of time you can spend in even the most fascinating of museums and still concentrate, while even the loveliest of parks can be dull if there is nothing curious or interesting to look at.

These are some of the places which will give you the best of both.

Hyde Park

Tube: Lancaster Gate, Marble Arch, Hyde Park Corner, Knightsbridge.

Hyde Park was a forest at the time of the Doomsday Book and Elizabeth I used to hunt here. But now with its neighbour Kensington Gardens, it is just a great and glorious expanse of grass and trees - 630 acres - for Londoners to enjoy. You are going to need comfortable shoes and lots of energy. Start at Hyde Park Corner and the museum at this end of the park, The Wellington Museum, Apsley House, W1. (See page 34). This was the home of the Iron Duke and now houses a splendid collection of Wellingtonia. Weekdays 10.00 a.m.-6.00 p.m. Sundays 2.30-6.00 p.m., children 5p, adults 10p. Here you will find Wellington's swords and decorations, with flags and shields and all the trophies of war, including some of the plunder he brought home displayed upstairs. A marvellous gallery of pictures includes three by Velasquez, and the Duke's portraits too, one very flattering Lawrence and the famous Goya Equestrian. The Wellington Arch opposite is the smallest Police station in London, but Constitution Arch now has no function except to act as a funnel for the Underpass and keep it clear of fumes. Just inside the park you will see yet another reminder of Wellington, the statue of Achilles which was erected in his honour and cast from cannon taken in his victories. As you walk west you may be lucky and see the Household Cavalry returning from Horse Guards to their barracks at Knightsbridge (about 10.00 a.m. and 11.45 a.m.). On their way they will pass Epstein's stunning statue of Pan (the God of forests not Peter Pan) with a group of people and a dog dashing wildly in the park.

Now head north across Rotten Row (which is the smartest place to ride in London) and on towards the Serpentine, London's famous and favourite lake, built for Queen Caroline in 1730. Here you can hire a boat if you are in the money (10.00 a.m.-3.30 p.m. all year, 25p an hour, 50p deposit and children must be accompanied by an adult) or rest at one of the two cafes. Here you can swim and sunbathe in summer (weekdays 3p for children, adults 7½p; weekends and holidays 5p and 12½p). In 1825 the ice was thick enough for a coach and four to be driven across it. Cross the beautiful old bridge with its views of the old towers of Westminster and the new one of the Hilton Hotel and walk across the park to Marble Arch. It was designed by Nash to be the gateway to Buckingham Palace, but was placed here instead although it was too narrow for traffic and the gates only open to royalty. It is amazing to think that this is the site of the infamous gallows of Tyburn. Here our blood-thirsty ancestors liked nothing better than to watch the public hangings and tortures; 200,000 came to see the highwayman Jack Shepherd die in 1724. Now the crowds come to shop in Oxford Street and Tyburn is abandoned to the traffic. On Sundays people throng to nearby Speakers' Corner where you can listen to and join in debates on all manner of subjects, crazy and otherwise.

Kensington Gardens

Tube: High Street Kensington, Queensway. A car park has just been opened by National Car Parks. Situated between Palace Gate and Kensington Palace Gardens.

Peter Pan country with starched nannies still pushing their prams along the Flower Walk. Enter the park by Palace Gate and go up the Broad Walk to Kensington Palace, the home of the London Museum. The Palace is part Wren, part Kent, and was first bought to be a Royal residence by William III. Royal relations live here now (Princess Margaret and Lord Snowdon) and except for a suite of state rooms, the Palace is private. It was here during a night in 1837 that

Princess Victoria was dramatically awakened to be told she was the Queen of England. The London Museum is full of fascinating relics of London from its earliest beginnings arranged in chronological order so you can travel through time from the city that existed in Saxon and Roman days through the Middle Ages and on to the present. There is a diorama of the Fire of London flickering realistically through the night and another of a Piccadilly traffic jam of the 1880's. A pennyfarthing stands alongside cases full of model horseless carriages and trams. There are doll's houses and Victoria's own dolls; evocative costumes from each period and the wonderful Cheapside Hoard - jewels thought to be the buried stock of a Jacobean jeweller.

Outside again in today's London there is the Round Pond where you can sail model boats or watch the expert fanatics with theirs. Occasionally they drain the pond to clean it and discover all the sad wrecks which failed to sail home. This is a good place to fish for tiddlers or to fly your kite as you run across to the statue of Physical Energy which is in the middle of Lancaster Walk. In the north-west corner of the Park, is a splendidly equipped children's playground, with a slide, and swings which were the gift of J.M. Barrie, whose Peter Pan statue waits for you a short way down the Serpentine, with Wendy in attendance and a host of rabbits and fairies carved around the base. Just outside the playground is the fantastic Elfin Oak with yet more marvellously carved animals and elves. South again to the Albert Memorial, with wide steps to sit on, as you gaze at Queen Victoria's beloved Albert clasping his catalogue of the Great Exhibition of 1851 under an ornate canopy of marble and bronze, inlaid with agate, onyx, jasper and cornelian. *Take your kite, boat, fishing net and jam jar.*

The Royal Botanic Gardens, Kew

Tube: Kew Gardens. British Rail: Kew Bridge. Open daily, except Christmas Day, from 10.00 a.m. till dusk NO DOGS ADMITTED SO LEAVE YOUR PETS BEHIND!

For 1p entrance fee you can spend the day exploring the most famous gardens in the world. Many trees are hundreds of years old and very rare, and there are orchids, bananas, roses and poppies from the Himalayas. A palace and a cottage stand in these 300 acres next to the Thames.

You will need to study the maps at the entrance carefully and decide what you most want to see as there are so many things. Close to the Main Gate is Kew Palace, which was built in 1631 and became a royal residence in 1781. Behind it is the Queen's Garden, a replica of a seventeenth century garden, planted only with those plants which were grown then; lovely old roses and herbs all marked with details of how they were used as medicines. There is a bench planted with camomile which smells delicious if you sit on it. Down the Broad Walk is the Orangery, which was built for Princess Augusta who started the gardens in 1759, where you can see oranges growing. Further on is the pond and the most beautiful greenhouse in the world, The Palm House built by Decimus Burton in 1884, which shelters a collection of palms, balsa, breadfruit, coffee and bananas which bear fruit regularly! It is tropically warm inside and smells delicious. You can climb right up into the roof on tiny white wrought-iron circular stairs and look down into the jungle below. Outside stand replicas of the Queen's Beasts which stood outside Westminster Abbey at the Coronation, and guarding the pond are two magnificent Chinese lions. To the north of the Palm House is the Water Lily House, where tropical lilies flower alongside the Sacred Lotus of the Buddhists and the Papyrus from which the ancient Egyptians made their paper. Outside again and westwards to the lake, where you can see lots of unusual wildfowl, including black swans, Muscovy duck and Magellan geese. Queens Cottage, in the south west corner of the park was built as a picnicing place for Queen Charlotte. The Pagoda has no function and you cannot climb up it but it is a marvellously decorative example of Chinoiserie. Near it you will see the flagstaff which was made from a single spar of Douglas Fir 225 ft high, and put up by the Royal Engineers. There is a wood museum in Cambridge Cottage, and in the General Museum by the pond there are displays on the history and work of Kew, and examples of botanical art alongside botanical exhibits.

Richmond Green, River and Park

Tube: Richmond. British Rail: Richmond.

Take your bikes or walk from the station across the village green towards the site of the old Palace of Richmond. Nothing remains of this once fabulous palace where Elizabeth I died but you can see the old arched Gateway to the Wardrobe where all those sumptuous clothes were stored. Go down Old Palace Lane and walk along the river to Petersham and the Express Dairy Farm (01-940-6211) where you can watch the cows being milked (about 3.30 p.m. every afternoon) and the calves being fed. Up the Star and Garter Hill, past the old soldiers who sit watching the traffic go by outside their Home, and into the Park. Richmond Park is enormous and wild and full of exciting wild life. Birds (the kestrels are back and hover hopefully overhead) and beasts; badgers and foxes (though we doubt if you will see them) chase after the pheasant, and deer graze everywhere. Be wary of the deer and treat them with respect, they can be dangerous if you annoy them. There are ponds to fish in and streams to paddle in. It is especially good at frogspawn time, while in the height of summer when the bracken is high you can hide in it and in the hundreds of hollow trees, and pretend you are deep in the country. There is a Woodland Garden, the Isabella Plantation which has a pretty stream running through hundreds of azaleas and rhododendrons and ducklings on the ponds in spring. You can watch Polo sometimes in the summer close to Roehampton Gate and promise yourself to ride here some day. White Lodge near Pen Ponds is the home of the Royal Ballet School which may explain all the children walking with their toes turned out. Pembroke Lodge near the Richmond Gate has lavatories, cafeteria and a restaurant. (Open weekdays from 10.00 a.m. until dusk in summer, closed in November, December and January except for weekends).

Battersea Park (01-228-2798)

Tube: Sloane Square. Bus 137. British Rail: Battersea Waterbus from Charing Cross or Westminster.

Battersea Park is not just the home of the Festival Gardens and Funfair, it boasts many other delights. Cross Chelsea Bridge past the splendid smoke-belching towers of the Power Station and into the Park. The Funfair stands temptingly by the river and the Main Gate. It opens at Easter and we think it best at weekends for fairs can be dreary without crowds of people. If you can resist the roundabouts and candyfloss, leave the music behind you and head for the Park itself. Here you can play tennis, kick a football about or watch an impromptu match, or make for the playgrounds in the south west corner. There is a paddling pool for younger children with a sandpit and swings, and a splendid adventure assault course for the toughs amongst you. In the middle of the park is a lake, loud with the quacking of ducks and honking of geese, and a sheltered garden which is a good place for a picnic out of the wind. Here they sometimes stage exhibitions of sculpture to join Henry Moore's Standing Figures. At the other end of the lake you can hire a boat (25p an hour, 50p deposit; weekends only in winter) or look at the rather sad deer in an enclosure there.

Just outside the park at 4 Battersea Park Road is the Dog's Home where stray dogs are cared for. If you have lost a dog or want to buy one, you can visit the kennels, but it is not a place for the soft-hearted who will want to rescue every old lag in the place and weep for the most endearing. Open Monday to Friday 9.30 a:m.-5.00 p.m. Saturday, Sunday and public holidays 2.00-4.00 p.m. Dogs are for sale from £4.00. Tel: 01 622 4454. Across the river, not far up Royal Hospital Road, is London's newest museum - The National Army Museum, (Monday to Saturday 1.00 a.m.-5.30 p.m. Sundays 2.00-5.30 p.m.) which covers the history of the British Army from the reign of Henry VII to the outbreak of the First World War. It also tells the story of the Indian Army and the Commonwealth armies. Magnificent pictures and uniforms, sets of orders and decorations. Pictures of uniforms for sale to colour when you get home at 3p each. Next door the Chelsea Royal Hospital (Monday to Saturday 10.00 a.m.-12 noon, 2.00 p.m.-6.00 p.m. Sundays 2.00-6.00 p.m.) Founded by Charles II as a hospital for aged or disabled soldiers and the home of the Chelsea Pensioners who gather in their scarlet summer uniforms on Founders Day, 29th May, to lay wreaths of oak on the statue of Charles II by Grinling Gibbons.

St. James's Park and Palace; Buckingham Palace.

Tube: St. James's, Hyde Park Corner, Green Park. Trafalgar Square, Victoria.

The grandest entrance to the Park is through the ceremonial Admiralty Arch and up the Mall, often brilliant with flags in honour of visiting VIPs, towards the glittering goldleaf-covered figure of Victory on top of the Victoria Memorial. One of the strangest of London's buildings is on the left, the Citadel. Built as a bombproof shelter in 1941 it housed the Naval Operations Room; now it is covered in camouflaging creepers and has an acre of lawn on the roof which it is the duty of the Superintendent of the Park to keep mown. Up the Mall on the right are the Carlton House Steps with the Grand Old Duke of York 124 ft high on his column of pink granite. There is a stairway inside the column but the door is kept firmly locked because people kept jumping off the top. Behind in Waterloo Place there is a statue of Florence Nightingale with her lamp.

Past Marlborough House is the old Tudor Palace of St. James's where Charles I spent the last night of his life before walking across the Park to die with such dignity and courage on the scaffold outside his Banqueting House in Whitehall. The Palace was the official residence of the sovereign from 1697 when the Palace of Whitehall burned down, until Queen Victoria decided to move up the Mall to Buckingham Palace. However it is from a balcony here that the Herald proclaims a new King and all ambassadors are still accredited to the Court of St. James's. The Palace is private but you may visit the Chapel Royal which is open for service on Sundays. The Guards march impassively up and down on the pavement outside with a great squeaking of boots, but if you want to see the Changing of the Guard you must hurry across to Buckingham Palace at 11.30 a.m. It is best to try to watch this ceremony in early spring or autumn when the tourist crowd is less thick than in the height of summer. Even if there are lots of people you can usually wriggle through to the front by the railings or ask a policeman if you may stand by the Gates, which is usually allowed except for during the minutes when the Guard marches in and out. If you have arrived early and there is still space there is a good view from the Victoria Memorial, where the figures of Truth, Motherhood and Justice are in attendance upon Her Majesty. The band plays, the Standard flies high above the Queen's Brigade of Guards when she's at home, the cameras click and the ghost of Christopher Robin goes home with Alice. The public is not allowed into the Palace except the Queen's Gallery where treasures from the royal palaces are on show. As the Queen owns one of the richest private collections of paintings, jewels, furniture and tapestries in the world, the exhibitions are fabulous. The entrance is in Buckingham Palace Road and it is open during exhibitions. Tuesday to Saturday 11.00 a.m.-5.00 p.m. including Easter Monday and Bank Holidays. Sundays 2.00-5.00 p.m. Admission, children and old-age pensioners 5p, adults 15p.

A little further down the road is the gateway to the Royal Mews, where on Wednesdays and Thursdays from 2.00-4.00 p.m. you can see all the Queen's horses and her carriages too. Admission, children 5p, adults 15p. Here are stables with every piece of equipment gleaming to match the sheen on the horses and the glitter of the State Coaches and Coronation Coach. Back in the park and just inside the gates, are a childrens' playground and lavatory. The park's lake is bright with ducks and geese which you can identify on notice boards at the far end by the teahouse. It is a wonderful place for birdwatching with many rare species, including a black swan and the famous pelicans which have been here, except in wartime, ever since the Russian Ambassador gave a present of a pair to Charles II. They are fed at 4.00 p.m. on the lawn near the old Birdkeeper's Lodge.

JAUNTS AND JOLLITIES

'Jaunts and jollities' are for those occasions when you are being treated to a special outing. Some are cheap, but provide lots of different things to see and do, and some are more expensive. To help you plan what you can afford to do, we have listed not only the admission fees, but also the additional charges for the extras that you are likely to want to visit, for instance the Children's Zoo at the London Zoo. Many places positively welcome large parties and have special reduced rates and catering services for them, so if you are planning a huge birthday party or can gang up with several other families for a celebration, you can cut costs drastically, and have a lot of fun doing so. Although most of these suggestions are best for fine days, you can find shelter at most places should it start to pour with rain. The two first mentioned outings are London's best wet weather entertainments.

Madame Tussaud's, Marylebone Road, NW1.(01-935-6861).

Tube: Baker Street. Open 10.00 a.m.-6.00 p.m. Closed Christmas Day. Admission children 35p, adults 70p. Double ticket to both Tussauds and Planetarium, children 40p, adults 85p. Restaurant and Snack Bar.

'There was an old woman called Tussaud
Who loved the grand folk in "Who's Who" so
That she made them in wax
Both their front and their backs
And asked no permission to do so'

So rhymed Punch in 1919. The 'grand folk' portrayed in this extraordinary and unique collection of waxworks include Bismark, and Bardot, Caesar and Chichester, Hitler and Hitchcock, Napoleon and Nureyev, Talleyrand and Twiggy, amongst an assortment of Kings and Queens, Popes and politicians, pop stars and poisoners. There is the Grand Hall full of the famous and Tableaux showing favourite scenes from history. 'Heroes' are displayed against marvellous backgrounds of suitable props, with special lighting and sound effects. They are retired to the storerooms when the public tires of them, a fate which has just befallen the figure of George Best. 'The Battle of Trafalgar', as it happened, is real theatre. You are engulfed by the sound of battle. You smell the sea and the tar and the rope, hear the bells tolling for the dead mingled with the victory peal, as they once rang for Nelson and his victory. The Chamber of Horrors will delight the ghouls amongst you, with its portraits of murderers, and its guillotines and gallows. We ourselves had nightmares for weeks afterwards, and loathed every minute of it, so the fainthearted be warned. On the other hand some children absolutely revel in it. The 13-year-old Princess Victoria instructed her aunt to write a letter of thanks to Tussauds after a visit to the exhibition. "We have been afforded much amusement and gratification"! You too?

The London Planetarium, Marylebone Road, NW1 (01-486-1121)

Tube: Baker Street. Open Monday-Friday 10.00 a.m. 6.00 p.m. Saturdays and Sundays 11.00 a.m.-6.00 p.m. Closed Christmas Day. Admission, children 20p, adults 35p. Double ticket to both Tussauds and the Planetarium, children 40p and adults 85p.

Under the great hemispherical dome of the Planetarium, you can sit and study the universe of the stars with an astronomer for a guide. It is just like being out of doors on a clear night as you watch the sun, moon and planets follow their correct paths across the star-studded night. But here you have an expert to explain the mystery of it all and not just another mother saying "I expect it's the Great Bear". The amazingly accurate and realistic reproduction of the heavens is produced by an enormous instrument, the £70,000 Zeiss Planetarium projector which produces images of the celestial bodies so that they are accurate in size, brightness and position, relative to each other. There are four different programmes: "A Year and a Day" is shown on Sundays and Mondays, "Journey into Space" on Tuesdays and Fridays, "Beyond the Moon" on Wednesdays and Saturdays, and "Captives of the Sun" on Thursdays.

FUN AT THE FAIR

Battersea Fun Fair and Festival Gardens, Battersea Park, SW11.(01-228-2226)

Tube: Sloane Square. British Rail: Queen's Road. Battersea Park. By river, frequent boats from Westminster Pier. Car Park and restaurants. The Park and gardens are open daily. The Fun Fair is open from Easter to September. Weekdays, Easter to July 2.00 p.m.-11.00 p.m. Sundays 12.00 p.m.-11.00 p.m. July to September, weekdays 1.00 p.m.-11.00 p.m. Sundays, 12.00 a.m.-11.00 p.m. Closing times may vary depending on weather. Admission to Fun Fair and Children's Zoo 5p and parties are welcome.

All the fun of the fair with roundabouts, big wheel the rotor, a water shute, and ghost trains, but the Big Dipper is being removed after a serious accident. The sideshows and candy floss have been joined by the new clowns and performers, the dolphins. The Dolphinarium is now the great attraction. You can walk high in the trees along the Tree Walk and glimpse the boats on the river beyond. The Children's Zoo gives rides on ponies and donkeys and there are lots of strokable domestic pets and farm animals.

Other fairs visit the parks and commons of London at various times throughout the summer.

Hampstead Heath, NW3

Tube: Hampstead, Golders Green

Two fairs are held on the Heath, one on the East Heath, one at Spaniards. They take place every Easter, Spring and August Bank Holidays.

Blackheath, SE10.

British Rail: Blackheath

There is a fair every Easter, Spring and August Bank Holiday.

Wormwood Scrubs, Du Cane Road, W12

Tube: East Acton

There is a fair every Spring, Easter and August Bank Holiday.

Putney Common, SW15

Tube: Putney Bridge. British Rail: Putney, Barnes.

The fair is on Lower Common, Lower Richmond Road in May.

Wimbledon Common, SW19

Tube: Wimbledon

The fair is by Rushmere Pond in June (in 1973 it is from June 1 to 9th).

Chessington Zoo, Chessington, Surrey (Epsom 78). (27227).

British Rail: Chessington South. Open every day 9.30 a.m.-dusk. Winter 10.00 a.m.-4.00 p.m. There are restaurants, cafeteria, fish & chips, refreshment kiosks and a car park. Admission, children 20p, adults 35p. Winter admission, November to February, children 7½p, adults 15p. Pets Corner 3p for everyone. Aquarium 3p, and push chairs for hire are 13p. Parties welcome. Circus: daily for two weeks from Good Friday, then weekends until Whitsun, then daily till mid-September. There is one performance at 3.30 p.m. or two performances at 2.00 p.m. and 4.00 p.m. Circus, children 10p, adults 20p.

Chessington has a Fun Fair, Boating Lake, a Model Village, Punch and Judy, a Circus and two miniature railways. One of the latter boasts a locomotive which is a half scale model of Stephenson's rocket. In gardens of 65 acres you can also have pony rides, visit the Aquarium and Pet's Corner, and amongst it all see the animals. Over a thousand animals are kept here, and although it is not at all on the same scale as the London Zoo or Whipsnade, they have a good collection, with lions and tigers, leopards, giraffe and sealions, and they are awaiting the arrival of a new baby elephant.

The London Zoo, Regent's Park, NW1 (01-722-3333/ 3544).

Tube: Baker Street, Camden Town. Car Park. Open every day, in summer from 9.00 a.m. in November to March from 10.00 a.m. Closed Christmas Day. Admis-

sion, children 30p, adults 50p, on Mondays, children 20p, adults 40p. Aquarium and Children's Zoo, children 5p, and adults 10p. Parties welcome. Push chairs 15p with 15p deposit. There is a First-Aid post, with facilities for mothers and babies, a restaurant and cafeteria. In summer there is a Wimpy Bar, autobars and kiosks. There is a playground. The zoo shop sells films, and a Guide at 20p which is well worth it.

Quite impossible to decide what to see first as everyone has a different favourite among the 6,000 animals which live here. Since Chi-Chi, the Giant Panda's death, I suppose Guy the Gorilla must be the most famous, with that great escapologist, Goldie the Golden Eagle a close second. New buildings are going up all the time. The Elephant and Rhino pavilion looks rather like a great pachyderm itself and the new Ape and Monkey House makes watching all that monkey business much easier. The Snowdon Aviary with its cantilevered bridge takes you right in amongst the birds so that you can almost touch a sacred ibis on its nest. A favourite place, apart from the Gibbon enclosure, is the 'Moonlight World' section of the Charles Clore Pavilion where the nocturnal animals are deceived into thinking it is time for action by the reversing of night and day. There is an otter pool, with waterfall and underwater window so that you can watch them swim. More aquatic displays when the sealions are fed and in the aquarium where you can see sea horses, and electric eels. The great cats always seem to have a cub or so about, and are waiting for their new enclosures. There are donkey and pony rides in the Children's Zoo where you can stroke rabbits and guinea pigs, sheep, goats, and maybe watch chicks hatching in the incubators. There are chimp intelligence tests, and a tea party too. You can ride the camels and have llama or pony trap rides for 3p. At the entrances are notices telling you of any new babies or animals of special interest, and the times when feeding takes place.

XYZ Club for Young Zoologists

For £1.00 a year you get a badge and membership card, six free admission tickets to London Zoo and Whipsnade, special lectures and films, and the Zoo magazine. For those between the ages of 9 to 18.

TRIPS ON THE REGENTS CANAL

Zoo Waterbus, Little Venice, London Zoo. (01-285-6101).

Tube: Paddington, Warwick Avenue. Open Easter to October.

The water bus takes visitors to the London Zoo from Little Venice, and from the Zoo back again, or you can join a round trip if there is a boat available. The single fare includes Zoo admission. The Little Venice landing stage is in Warwick Crescent.

Little Venice to the Zoo: Monday to Saturday departures hourly, on the hour, from 10.00 a.m.-5.00 p.m. Sundays 10.00 a.m.-6.00 p.m. Single fare including admission to the Zoo, children 40p, adults 70p.

London Zoo to Little Venice: Monday-Saturday departures hourly, on the hour, 11.00 a.m.-5.00 p.m. Sundays 10.30 a.m.-1.30 p.m. and 2.00-6.00 p.m. Fare children 10p and adults 20p.

Round trip from London Zoo: When a boat is available, Monday to Saturday hourly, on the hour from 11.00 a.m.-3.00 p.m. Sundays 2.00-6.00 p.m. Fare, children 13p, adults 26p.

Round trip from Little Venice: When a boat is available, Monday to Saturday hourly, on the hour, from 10.00 a.m.-4.00 p.m. Sundays 10.00 a.m.-5.00 p.m. Fare, children 13p, adults 26p.

You voyage along the Regent's Canal from the landing stage in Little Venice, which faces Browning's Island, and through the Maida Hill tunnel. Built in 1816, it is 272 yards long, and has no towpath, so that horses had to be led over the top until they were eventually replaced by tugs. The canal flows through Regent's Park and under Blow Up Bridge, which takes its name from an explosion which occurred one night in 1874. A barge laden with gunpowder blew up just as it passed underneath the iron bridge, and only the deep cutting prevented widespread destruction. The bridge was rebuilt on its original columns but the scores made by the horses' towing lines are now on the 'wrong' side.

Jason's Trip, Argonaut Gallery, Blomfield Road, W9 (01-286-3428)

Tube: Warwick Avenue, Paddington. Open Easter to October. Fare, children 25p, adults 65p.

The *Jason* is a traditional narrow boat, 80 years old and most beautifully decorated with the special livery peculiar to canal boats. She tows a 'butty', the *Serpens,* behind her on the two hour voyage along the canal from Little Venice, through the Park to Camden Town and back again. There are three trips during the day and delicious food is served on board. The boat is licenced throughout the day too, which may please some of your exhausted parents, and there is a commentary so that you don't miss any of the landmarks on the way. There is also an evening trip, with entertainment first at the Argonaut Gallery, then supper on board while moored in Regent's Park.

Departures at 11.00 a.m. with a three course lunch for 70p, and at 2.00 p.m. with high tea at 70p. The 4.30 p.m. departure also has high tea for 70p. Evening trips including supper and entertainment are £2.50.

'Jenny Wren' Trips, 250 Camden High Street, NW1. (01-485-6210)

Tube: Camden Town

By narrow boat from Camden Town to Little Venice and return is 90 minutes. Fare: children accompanied 15p, adults 30p. From Easter until 29 May Saturday and Sundays at 2.00 p.m. and 3.30 p.m. From 30th May to 21st July daily at 2.00 p.m. and 3.30 p.m. From 22nd July to 3rd September daily at 11.00 a.m., 2.00 p.m. and 3.30 p.m. Special Saturday trips 6.30-10.30 p.m. until 9th September, with pub visit, fare 60p and Fridays 7.00-10.00 p.m. fare 50p. Groups and private hire by arrangement. It is advisable to book in advance.

Regent's Canal Towpath

The canal is gradually being opened up again, and you can now walk along two newly opened stretches of towpath, for one mile between Lisson Grove Bridge and the Primrose Hill Bridge and for one third of a mile between the Great Western Road Bridge and Harrow Road Bridge. No children under ten are admitted unless accompanied by an adult.

SYON HOUSE

Syon Park, Brentford, Middlesex. (01-560-3225)

Tube: Hammersmith. Bus: 267. British Rail: Waterloo to Syon Lane. Restaurant, cafeteria, bar and snacks. Car Park. House: opening times vary, check by telephone. Admission children 10p, adults 30p. Gardens: open daily except Christmas Day and Boxing Day, summer 10.00 a.m.-6.00 p.m., winter 10.00 a.m.-4.00 p.m. Admission, children 16½p, adults 22p. Aquarium and Aviary, children 5½p, adults 11p. 'History on Wheels' Car Museum, children 15p, adults

10p. London Transport Collection, children 15p, adult
25p.

Syon House is the London home of the Duke o
Northumberland. The house, which is basically Tudor
was completely remodelled by Adam in 1770 and the
interior is one of the most elegant in England. A
beautiful lake lies in the grounds which were land
scaped by the famous 'Capability Brown' with hund
reds of rare trees and beautiful gardens. The Grea
Conservatory is said to have served as a model for the
Crystal Palace, and now houses an aquarium and ar
aviary of tropical and humming birds, the London
Transport Collection of vintage buses, trams and under
ground trains has moved here from its old home in
Clapham because the rest of the Transport Museum
collection is being taken to York. The oldest vehicle
in the collection which actually drove along London'
streets is the 'Times' knifeboard omnibus, the firs
horsebus to carry passengers on the roof. The bus had
to be called in and refitted with 'decency boards' to
stop pedestrians looking up the women's skirts! There
are many other rare vehicles and things connected
with them, such as clippies' uniforms from before the
First World War, and ticket punches. The History or
Wheels exhibition is a museum of vintage and vetera
cars, so transport enthusiasts can have a field day here
While they are doing so, those of you with green
fingers might like to inspect the famous Garden Centre
where hundreds of shrubs and plants are grown for sale

HEATHROW AIRPORT

Bath Road, Hounslow, Middlesex. (01-759-4321)

Tube: Hounslow West and express bus. British Rai
Feltham and bus. Spectators' Car Park on Northside
of Airport from which London Transport provide
regular shuttle service to the Central Area Bus Terminu.
during the summer. Visitors are asked not to use the

Central Area Car Parks during the summer as passengers have priority. It is advisable to telephone National Car Parks, 01-759-7260, to check whether the shuttle service is operating before you leave home. No dogs are admitted.

Spectator Roof Gardens: Open daily in January, November and December from 10.00 a.m. to 4.30 p.m. In February and March from 10.00 a.m.-5.00 p.m. In April and May from 10.00 a.m.-6.00 p.m. In June, July and August from 10.00 a.m.-7.00 p.m. In September from 10.00 a.m.-6.00 p.m., and October from 10.00 a.m.-5.00 p.m. On Sundays and Bank Holidays during March, May, July, August and September it is open for one extra hour in the evening. All of which is what you might call fairly complicated! Admission 5p for children, adults 15p for the whole day. Licensed cafeteria, amusement arcade, shops, playground and shelter if it rains. Parties are welcome.

London Airport is the busiest international Airport in the world, and on busy summer days handles over 900 aircraft movements. You can watch all this activity from the roofs of the Queen's Building and Terminal 2. A commentary relayed over the public address system will tell you the destination and points of origin of the various aircraft, identify the aircraft types, and describe the livery of the various airlines. Lots of other information too for those aeroplane addicts whose one idea of bliss is to listen to the scream of jet engines all day.

BIRDS' EYE VIEWING

Shell Centre Public Viewing Gallery, Shell Centre, York Road, SE1. (01-934-1234)

Tube: Waterloo. British Rail. Car Park. Open April to October Mondays to Fridays from 10.00 a.m.-5.00 p.m. Admission, children 5p, adults 15p. No unaccompanied children. Closed Saturdays, Sundays and Public Holidays.

The Viewing Gallery of the Shell Centre is on the 25th floor of one of the largest office blocks in Europe. You reach it by a lift which travels at 13 feet a second to the 24th floor, then walk up two flights of steps to find yourself 317 feet above London. The view is tremendous and there are panoramic drawings and a telescope to help identify the landmarks. It is a good idea to visit the gallery before a trip on the river or before a visit to the nearby Festival Hall, or HMS Discovery.

Post Office, Tower, 60 Cleveland Street, W1.(01-636 -3133)

Tube: Goodge Street, Warren Street, Regent's Park, Great Portland Street. No parking facilities, and this is a difficult area in which to find a meter. Open weekdays from 9.30 a.m.-9.30 p.m., Saturdays and Sundays from 9.00 a.m.-9.30 p.m. Admission children 10p, adults 20p. There is a souvenir shop. Unaccompanied children under 14 are not admitted. There is a 'Top of the Tower Restaurant'. (01-636-3000).

At the moment the Observation Platforms are closed for repairs following a terrorists' attempt to blow the tower even further skyhigh, so telephone first to find out whether it is open again. The restaurant is open, but, as the basic minimum charge per person is £2.90 you will need to be very rich or very persuasive to enjoy the view as it rotates about the central core of the tower at the rate of 2½ times an hour.

This is the tallest building in London and its finest vantage point, but also the symbol of the modern Post Office which uses special techniques in telephone, teleprinter, television and computer communications. Its height is essential for it must carry aerials high above obstructions to provide a clear path for about 150,000 simultaneous circuits carrying television programmes, telephone conversations and computer data between London and the rest of the country. Two lifts carry 14 passengers at 1,000 feet a minute to the three observation platforms, the highest of which is 499 feet above ground level. The total height of the Tower, including the mast, is 620 ft, and the restaurant is at 520 ft. Binoculars and large photographic panoramas help in your search for landmarks in this most fantastic view of London. Downstairs again there is an automatic question-and-answer service in the foyer, which will help sort out the technicalities baffling you. You can also send postcards from the Tower which will be specially postmarked. Combine a visit to the Tower with one to Pollock's Toy Museum just down the road, or with a visit to the British Museum.

WAR GAMES

London is a marvellous place for inspecting the troops. You can watch the Queen's men as they drill on the barrack square or Change the Guard at the Palace, or see them in action on State occasions and at special displays, when the public can also examine their equipment. There are many museums packed with relics from the past and examples of present day life in the Army, Navy and Air Force.

Changing the Guard.

This must surely be London's favourite and most famous ceremony. You can watch the drill that produces such polished performances at Wellington and Chelsea Barracks. The men wear their bearskins at practice because they must get used to the weight. Each cap weighs 2½ lbs but gets much heavier in the rain. Wellington Barracks, Birdcage Walk, SW1; Chelsea Barracks, Chelsea Bridge Road, SW1. You cannot enter the Barracks, but you can watch through the railings, there are no specified times for drilling, so it is not worth a special expedition but it is fun to watch if you happen to be passing.

Buckingham Palace

Tube: St. James's, Victoria, Hyde Park Corner, Ceremony at 11.30 a.m. daily.

The Queen's Guard is provided by the Brigade of Guards, although at times other regiments alternate duty with the Guards Division. The guard marches behind a band from either Wellington or Chelsea Barracks and arrives in the forecourt at about 11.30 a.m. every morning. The ceremony lasts about half an hour. The Guards carry the Queen's Colour of crimson when the Court is in London; otherwise, the Regimental Colour. In very bad weather there is no ceremony. Policemen are very helpful about allowing children to wriggle through to the front of the crowd, but try to avoid the busy summer tourist season.

Horse Guards, Whitehall.

Tube: Trafalgar Square, Strand. Ceremony at 11.00 a.m. on weekdays. 10.00 a.m. on Sundays.

The Queen's Life Guard is provided by the Household Cavalry. It is changed every morning at 11.00 a.m. by either the Life Guards or the Blues and Royals. The guard is inspected on foot at 4.00 p.m. The forecourt is very small so arrive early for a good view.

The Guards Division

The Guards Division consists of five regiments who all wear scarlet tunics and bearskin caps. The *Grenadiers* wear a white plume on the left and single-spaced buttons in contrast to the *Coldstreams* who have a scarlet plume on the right with buttons set in twos. The *Scots Guards* have no plumes and their buttons are in threes, while the *Irish Guards* have a blue plume on the right and their buttons in fours. The *Welsh Guards* wear a green and white plume on the left, with buttons in groups of five.

The Household Cavalry

The Household Cavalry is made up of two regiments, the Life Guards and the Blues and Royals. From these the Mounted Regiment of the Household Cavalry, which provides the Queen's Life Guard, is formed. The Life Guards wear red tunics and white helmet plumes and the sheepskins on their saddles are white; whereas the sheepskins of the Blues and Royals are black and they wear blue tunics with red plumes. They usually wear the cuirass, the breast and back plate, only when they are mounted. The Household Cavalry horses are all black, except for the greys of the trumpeters and the skewbalds of the mounted drummers.

Firing Salutes

Guns are fired in salute to mark special occasions such as the anniversary of the Queen's accession, Royal Family birthdays, the official Birthday of the Sovereign in June and the State Opening of Parliament. The arrivals of visiting Royalty or Heads of State are also marked by salutes. Royal Salutes are fired in Hyde Park by the King's Troop, Royal Horse Artillery, usually at noon; while the salutes at the Tower of London are by the Honourable Artillery Company and take place at 1 p.m. A special gunpowder mixture is used to ensure that the puffs of smoke are white. Look for advertisements of the special events in the Press and on London Transport posters.

The King's Troop, Royal Horse Artillery

This is the only remaining mounted unit in the Royal Artillery. Their horse-drawn gun carriages are a magnificent sight, especially at full gallop (see Royal

Tournament). The full-dress uniform consists of hussar pattern jacket of blue with a great deal of gold piping and breeches with a broad stripe of red. Their new barracks are in St. John's Wood.

The Honourable Artillery Company

The oldest regiment in the British Army, it dates from the sixteenth century when they were, as they still are, volunteers. The Company has its own coat of arms, a unique privilege granted in 1629 and furnish a Guard of Honour on certain State occasions in the City of London when they march with swords drawn and colours flying to the beat of the drum. The artillery division is responsible for salutes at the Tower.

ACTION STATIONS

Trooping the Colour

Trooping the Colour takes place on Horse Guards Parade on the first or second Saturday in June, in honour of the Queen's Birthday. A splendid spectacle as Her Majesty rides to inspect her troops. Rehearsals for the event are held on the two preceeding Saturdays, and it is sometimes easier to get tickets for these. Application for tickets should be sent to *The Brigade Major, Household Division, Horse Guards, Whitehall, London, SW1. 01-930-4466.*

Beating Retreat

Horse Guards is also the scene for the ceremony of Beating Retreat. It is being performed on two occasions this year. On 22nd, 23rd and 24th May the Brigade of Guards beat retreat, and the Royal Marines take over on 11th, 12th and 13th June. Applications for tickets should be sent to the *Advance Booking Office, 144 Charing Cross Road, WC2. 01-437-4236.*

The Royal Tournament

The Royal Tournament is held annually during July at Earl's Court in aid of Service Charities. The programme presented by the three Services evolved from the original "Grand Tournament and Assault-at-Arms" in 1881 and is different every year. This year from July 11th to 28th the Fleet Air Arm will be showing how a frigate armed with helicopters and missiles can locate and destroy any hostile intruder; the Royal Marines will demonstrate their modern techniques in Arctic warfare, and the Royal Air Force will perform their latest drills in training free-fall parachutists. The Army Physical Training Corps will dazzle us with their gymnastics and the crowd will roar a welcome for two items always on the agenda; the thrilling Musical Drive by the King's Troop, Royal Horse Artillery, as they gallop their gun carriages in frightening manoeuvres and the exciting Naval Field Gun Competition, a race between two teams to dismantle a gun then reassemble it on the other side of a deep ditch which they must cross. Marvellous martial music from Massed Bands, and displays from regiments from the Commonwealth add to a very long and varied programme. This year, the visitors are the Royal Barbados Police Band who have a special steel band section. After the show there are various stands to visit and you can also see the stables.

Applications for tickets to *The Royal Tournament, 166 Piccadilly, W1. Box Office 01-499-2639.*

SUNDAY SERVICES

Guards Chapel, Wellington Barracks, Birdcage Walk, SW1. (01-930-4466 Ext: 298).

A beautiful modern building with the six chapels dedicated to the five regiments of the Foot Guards and to the Household Cavalry. The Household Brigade Cenotaph contains seven Books of Remembrance. A military band plays before the service and accompanies many of the hymns. Sundays 10.45 a.m. for Matins at 11.00 a.m. The Chapel is also open on weekdays from 10.00 a.m.-4.00 p.m.

St. Clement Danes, Strand, WC2. (01-242-8282).

The official church of the Royal Air Force, with 735 crests of the squadrons cut in slate set in the floor and beautiful Books of Remembrance to see after Matins at 11 a.m. On a Sunday in March each year, oranges and lemons are distributed to the children of the Parish. The bells which play the famous nursery rhyme tune have been restored after war damage.

Chapel Royal of St. Peter Ad Vinicula, Tower of London, EC3.

Although the Tower itself is closed on Sunday mornings, the Chapel is open for worship. The service is at 11.15 a.m.

MUSEUMS

The Royal Air Force Museum, Aerodrome Road, Hendon, NW9. (01-205 -2266)

Tube: Colindale. Open Monday-Saturday 10.00 a.m.-6.00 p.m. Sundays 2.00-6.00 p.m. Admission free. Restaurant. Car Park.

Opened by the Queen in 1972, this modern museum houses the latest jet fighter alongside forty-two other full-scale aircraft and parts of airships, balloons and kites to demonstrate the history of military aviation. These and other relics are displayed chronologically together with electronically operated models showing life in the Royal Air Force today. At the push of a button you can see a day in the life of a typical Royal

Air Force station, or a model showing communication systems or tactical operations. The most exciting exhibit must be the flight simulator in which you can test your reactions to flying an aeroplane. A cinema shows clips from literally hundreds of films concerned with aviation, from the bombing sequence in the Dam Busters to some of the latest in flight. It is a very exciting collection imaginatively produced, and presented for maximum entertainment value.

HMS Belfast: details in *The River.* (Greenwich Section)
The Tower of London: details in *Sightseeing*
National Army Museum: details in *Parks and Palaces.*
Wellington Museum: details in *Parks and Palaces.*
National Maritime Museum Greenwich: details in *The River.* (Greenwich section)
Imperial War Museum: details in *Museums*
Wallace Collection: details in *Museums*
Artillery Museum Woolwich: details in *Museums*

SPORTING SPECIAL

For the energetic participant and slothful spectator alike, London is a great centre for sport. Clubs abound and the best idea initially is to contact the association of whatever sport interests you, and they will put you in touch with a local club.

The Central Council of Physical Recreation, 160 Great Portland Street, W1. (01-580-9092)

The Council exists to give 'help and advice to individuals and organisations in the field of physical recreation' and will give details of local organizers of any sport.

The Crystal Palace Sports Centre, SE19. (01-778-0131)

This is London's National Sports Centre and the largest in the country, acting as a training centre for clubs, coaches and individuals in over 50 sports. It has teaching and diving pools as well as an Olympic size swimming pool. There is an indoor arena for tennis, basketball and badminton, squash courts and an indoor cricket school. There is a dry-ski slope, Tartan track and more outside tennis courts. A fee of 25p is charged for a year's entry to the Centre, and small charges are made for use of the equipment and teaching facilities. Important national and international events are staged here, and include swimming, water polo, athletics and basketball. Cycling events are held on the road circuit in the park.

Empire Stadium and Pool, Empire Way, Wembley, Middlesex. (01-902-1234)

Famous for the Cup Final which is held here, also for international football, hockey, Gaelic football and hurling matches, and the final of the Rugby League, wrestling, boxing, ice hockey, skating, tennis, basketball, netball, cycle races and the Horse of the Year Show take place here too, and the International Horse Show.

Royal Albert Hall, Kensington Gore, SW7.(01-589-8212)

The hall is for professional and amateur boxing, wrestling and gymnastics.

Athletics: AAA Championships and international meetings are held at Crystal Palace, amateur meetings at the *Copthall Stadium, Hendon, Eton Manor, the Polytechnic Stadium, Chiswick* and at Tooting Bec and Twickenham. The *Amateur Athletic Association 26 Park Crescent, W1. (01-580-3498) gives information* about clubs and a list of events.

Badminton: *Badminton Association of England, 81a High Street, Bromley, Kent. (01-460-5722).* The England Championships are held at Wembley in March with tournaments at Wimbledon, Epsom, Eltham, Crystal Palace and Sydenham. The All England Junior

Championship takes places at Wimbledon in January.

Basketball: *Amateur Basketball Association, 32 Long gord Avenue, Bedfont, Feltham, Middlesex. (01-460-5722).* The best events are the National Championships at Crystal Palace, and the visit of the Harlem Globe Trotters to Wembley which is better than that cartoon on television.

Boxing: *Amateur Boxing Association, 10 Story's Gate, SW1 (01-930-9207).* The ABA championship held in April or May at Wembley. Other fights are at Wembley, Olympia, Earl's Court, Lime Grove and the Royal Albert Hall.

Canoeing: *British Canoeing Union, 26 Park Crescent, W1. (01-580-4710).* The Thames Youth Venture works in association with the National Voluntary Organisations and Local Education Authorities to provide facilities for canoeing, sailing and rowing for young Londoners. You can get details from your local Youth Office or from the following bases:-

Barn Elms Boathouse, Putney (01-788-9472) - rowing.
Raven's Ait, Surbiton, Surrey (01-977-2479) - sailing and canoeing.
Thames Young Mariners, Ham, Richmond, Surrey (01-940-5550) - sailing, canoeing.
Leaside Young Mariners Boating Centre, springfield Park, Hackney, E5 (01-806-6887) - canoeing.
Welsh Harp Youth Sailing Base, Cool Oak Lane, Hendon NW9 (01-202-6672) - sailing, canoeing.

The Scout Association, 25 Buckingham Palace Road, SW1 (01-834-6005). The Sea Activities Committee will advise on all boating, canoeing and sea activities for members of the association.

The Sea Cadet Corps, Broadway House, The Broadway, SW19 (01-540-8222). This is for older children, They provide classes in seamanship, navigation, radio, electronics, and engineering, together with sailing, rowing and maintaining their boats.

Cricket: Dial 160 for the latest Test Scores. You can watch Test matches and County Cricket at Lord's and the Oval. Village green cricket is played on Putney Common, Richmond Green, Ham Common, Kew Green, Holland Park. Nets can be booked at some GLC Parks.

Lord's Cricket Ground, St. John's Wood Road, NW8 (01-289-8011/1615). The Ground of the MCC which is also the governing body for British cricket. There is a coaching scheme and coaching awards are given. The Test match is in June. The museum of cricket is open on match days from 10.30 a.m. until close of play.

The Oval, The Surrey Ground, Kennington Oval, SE11 (01-735-2424). There is a Test Match in August.

Gover Cricket School, 172 East Hill, SW81 (01-874-1796). Book well in advance for holiday cricket coaching. This applies too at the *Chiswick Indoor Cricket School, 5 Prince of Wales Terrace, W4 (01-994-5808).* There is also an indoor cricket school at Crystal Palace.

Cycling: *British Cycling Federation, 26 Park Crescent, W1 (01-636-4602).* Write for a list of clubs and events. Main events are held at the Crystal Palace Sports Centre. However, for the ordinary person, cycling is not to be recommended in London's traffic, but some suburbs and parks are good. You can take your bike on the Circle, Metropolitan and District Lines for half the adult fare, but avoid the rush hours, or you will be more than unpopular. If your parents want to come too, but haven't got bikes, they can hire them from *Savilles Cycle Stores, 97 Battersea Rise, SW11 (01-228-4279).*

Fencing: *Amateur Fencing Association, 83 Perham Road, W14 (01-385-7442).*

Football: *Football Association, 22 Lancaster Gate, W2.* Write for information. The F.A. Cup Final is held at Wembley in May, but it is almost impossible to get tickets unless you are a regular supporter. You can arrange to watch Football League teams practising by applying in advance to the managers of these London clubs:

Arsenal Stadium Football Club, Avenall Road, N5 (01-226-3312).
Chelsea Football Club, Stamford Bridge, Fulham Road, SW6 (01-385-5545).
Crystal Palace Football Club, Selhurst Park, SE15 (01-653-2223).
Queen's Park Rangers Football Club, Ellerlie Road W12 (01-743-3478).
Tottenham Hotspur Football Club, White Hart Lane, N17 (01-808-1020).
West Ham United, Boleyn Ground Green Street, E13 (01-472-0 704).
Fulham Football Club, Craven Cottage, Stevenage Road, SW6 (01-736-7035).

If you have been to a match, and are travelling home alone or with friends, it is sensible to remove your scarf and rosettes and so avoid any confrontation with rival supporters.

Gymnastics: Events are held at the Royal Albert Hall and at Crystal Palace. Information available from the

British Amateur Gymnastics Association, 26 Park Crescent, W1 (01-580-3249). Edward Sturges, 106 Pavilion Road, SW1 (01-235-4234) runs daily gymnastic classes for children from 3½ upwards.

Hockey: International matches are held at Wembley and Hurlingham Park. Information from *The Hockey Association, 26 Park Crescent W1 (01-580-4840)* and the *All England Women's Hockey Association, 45 Doughty Street, WC1 (01-405-7514)*.

Judo: *The Budokwai Judo Club, 4 Gilston Road, SW10 (01-370-1000)* is the premier judo club of Europe. There is also the *British Judo Association, 26 Park Crescent, W1 (01-580-7585)*.

Lacrosse: *All England Women's Lacrosse Association, 26 Park Crescent, W1 (01-636-1123)*.

Lawn Tennis: *The Lawn Tennis Association, Barons Court W14 (01-385-2366)* will supply a list of clubs and events, the best of which take place at the following places:

All England Lawn Tennis and Croquet Club, Church Road, SW19 (01-946-2244). The last week of June and the first week of July see the tennis world's top event staged here. Tickets for the Centre and No. 1 Court are allotted by ballot, so apply early. There are huge queues for tickets on the day and people sleep out all night to be first in the queue. If you go in the early evening you can usually buy tickets which have been returned. Sometimes people leaving will give you theirs. This is a great place for stargazing but frustrating if you can't watch the most exciting match and have to listen to the gasps of those who are doing so. *The Empire Pool, Wembley, Middlesex (01-902-1234)* holds the Covered Court Championship, usually in November or December. The *Hurlingham Club, Ranelagh Gardens, SW6 (01-736-8411)* holds the London

Hard Court Championships in April or May. *Queen's Club, Palliser Road, W14 (01-385-3421)* is where you can see the Wimbledon stars play before the Wimbledon events, and much more easily. *Slazenger School of Lawn Tennis, 17 Hall Road, St. John's Wood, NW8 (01-286-3955)* is good for coaching. There are public courts in about 60 of London's Parks. They are extremely cheap to play on. Details from the *Parks Department, Cavell House, 2a Charing Cross Road, WC2 (01-836-5464) Ext: 143)*.

Netball: *All England Netball Association, 26 Park Crescent, W1 (01-580-3459)*. Netball pitches can be booked in the GLC Parks if you have an adequate number of friends to make up a team.

Racing (horses): For a day out with all the fun of the fair and the excitement of the racing too, go to *DERBY DAY AT EPSOM* by British Rail from Waterloo or Victoria. Go on the downs, it is cheap and great fun. For *ASCOT* take British Rail from Waterloo. Go on the Heath, the inside of the track, during the Royal Meeting in June, and watch the Queen drive down the course at the head of a procession of carriages drawn by Windsor Greys with scarlet outriders.

Riding: The Royal International Horse Show is in July, the Horse of the Year Show is in October at Wembley. The Greater London Horse Show on Clapham Common, SW4, is in August. You can ride in Hyde Park, on Wimbledon Common, Putney Common and in Richmond Park. These are some of the stables at which you can hire a horse or be taught to ride:

L.G. Blums Riding School and Livery Stable, 32 Grosvenor Crescent Mews, SW1 (01-235-6846).
Civil Service Riding Club, 1 de Vere Mews, Canning Place, W8 (01-584-8955).

The Equestrian Centre, The Ridgeway, Mill Hill, NW7 (01959-3818) has an indoor school.
Ridgeway School of Equitation, 93 Ridgeway, Wimbledon, SW19 (01-946-7400).
School of Natural Equitation, Stag Lodge, Robin Hood Gate, Kingston Vale, SW15 (01-546-9863).
Roehampton Riding Stable, Priory Lane, Roehampton Gate, SW15(01-876-7089), no children under 12.

They are all expensive. The central stables charge about £2.50 an hour, the others about £1.50, but horses aren't cheap to run. Lessons will be extra.

Rowing: Events take place in spring and summer. The Oxford and Cambridge Boat Race from Putney to Mortlake, usually takes place in March or early April, and the Head of the River Race and the Schools Head of the River Race over much the same course a week or so before. Regattas are held at Brent, Chiswick, Hammersmith, Kingston, Putney, Richmond or Twickenham. *Amateur Rowing Association, 160 Great Portland Street, W1 (01-580-0854),* supplies details of these and clubs to join. Soo also under Canoeing for River activities including rowing.

Rugby Football: Internationals are played at the *Rugby Football Union Ground, Whitton Road, Twickenham, Middlesex,* and Rugby League finals at Wembley. Club rugby is great to watch and Seven-a-Sides provide a day's entertainment. Especially good is the Middlesex Sevens held in April at Twickenham. The following are some of the grounds.

London Welsh, The Old Deer Park, Kew Road, Richmond (01-940-2368).
Harlequin Football Club, Craneford Way, Twickenham (01-892-3080).
Wasps Football Club, Repton Avenue, Sudbury, Middlesex (01-902-4220).

Rosslyn Park, Upper Richmond Road, SW15 (01-876-1879).

Sailing: Easiest to join in if your parents are members of a sailing club because obviously clubs are unwilling to take responsibility for you in what can be a dangerous pastime. You might try the following clubs:

London Corinthian Sailing Club, Linden House, Upper Mall, W6 (01-748-3280).
Twickenham Yacht Club, Riverside, Twickenham (01-892-8487).
Tamesis Club, Broom Road, Teddington (01-977-3589).

Otherwise see the section on Canoeing, which includes advice on River activities.

Skating and Ice Skating: Tuition available at all rinks.
Queen's Ice Skating Club, Queen's Court, Queensway, W2 (01-229-0172) Open 10.00 a.m.-12.00, 2.00-5.00 p.m. and 7.00-10.00 p.m. Membership 15p, hire of skates 10p, children 20p morning, 25p afternoon. Adults 25p morning, 30p afternoon.
Richmond Ice Rink, Clevedon Road, East Twickenham, Middlesex (01-892-3646). Open 10.00 a.m.-12.15, 2.30-5.00 p.m. and 7.00-10.00 p.m. Admission 15p, hire of skates 5p for children. Adults, admission 30p, hire of skates 10p.
Silver Blades Ice Rink, 386 Streatham High Road, SW16 (01-769-7861). Open 10.00 a.m.-12.00, 2.30-5.00 p.m., 7.30-11.00 p.m. Daytime skating 25p including hire of skates. Evening prices vary between Monday 25p, to Saturday 40p and 10p extra for hire of skates.
National Skating Association of Great Britain, Charterhouse, EC1 (01-253-3824).

Roller Skating: *Alexandra Palace Roller Rink, Wood Green N22 (01-883-9711).* Saturdays 10.30 a.m.-12.30

15p admission and 15p for hire of roller skates.

Ski-ing: Not as unlikely as it sounds as there are several artificial slopes to practise on. *National Ski Federation of Great Britain, 118 Eaton Square, SW1 (01-235-8288)*, publish a list of dry-ski schools and will arrange holidays in Britain and abroad. All these places run classes:

> *Alexandra Palace Ski Centre Ltd., Alexandra Palace Grounds (01-888-2284).*
> *Crystal Palace Sports Centre, SE19 (01-778-0131)*
> *Simpson (Piccadilly) Ltd., Philbeach Hall, Philbeach Gardens, SW5 (01-734-2002).*
> *Lillywhites Dry Ski School, Piccadilly Circus, SW1 (01-920-3181).*
> *Gordon Lowes Ltd., 173 Sloane Street, SW1 (01-235-8484).*
> *Moss Bros Ltd, Bedford Street, WC2 (01-240-4567)*

Squash: *The Squash Rackets Association, 26 Park Crescent, W1 (01-636-6901).* The growth of squash as a sport is limited by the number of courts available. There are some at the Crystal Sports Centre, and others at *Holland Park, W11 (01-937-3390).*

Swimming: *Amateur Swimming Association, 64 Cannon Street, EC4 (01-236-4868).* The Association will give you details of swimming events, coaching and swimming tests. Most boroughs have swimming pools. *The National Sports Centre at Crystal Palace* has a superb Olympic size pool, diving and teaching pools. with excellent teaching facilities. Other indoor pools include:

> *Buckingham Palace Road, SW1 (01-730-9030)*
> *Caledonian Road, N1 (01-837-6964)*
> *Chelsea Manor Street, SW3 (01352-6985)*
> *Great Smith Street, SW1 (01-222-4549)*
> *Ironmonger Road, EC1 (01-253-4011)*

Kensal Road, W10 (01-969-0772)
Marshall Street (01-437-7665)
Merlin Street, WC1 (01-837-1313)
The Oasis, Endell Street, WC2 (01-836-9555) also
has an outdoor pool.
Porchester Street (01-229-3226)
Putney Baths, Upper Richmond Road, SW15 (01-789-1124). Separate pool for beginners.
Richmond Baths, Old Deer Park, Richmond (01-940-8461) has an outdoor pool, and paddling
pool tool. Good place for sunbathing.
Seymour Place, W1 (01-723-8018)

Admission charges are all about 5p and cheaper for
the outdoor pools in many of the London parks.

Table Tennis: Tournaments are held at *Crystal Palace,
Wembley,* and the Royal Albert Hall. The *English
Table Tennis Association, 26 Park Crescent, W1 (01-580-6312)* will give information about clubs and
coaching. This seems to be the way to pave future
Anglo-Chinese relations, so get cracking if you want a
trip to the Great Wall.

Tenpin Bowling: *The British Tenpin Bowling Association, 202 Lower Clapton Road, E5 (01-985-2115)*
will provide a list of clubs and events. Wembley
Stadium stages the annual championships. Practise at
the *Mecca, 142 Streatham Hill, SW2 (01-674-5251)*
Open 10.00 a.m.-6.00 p.m. Admission 5p plus 2p for
shoes, adults 10p. Open 6.00 p.m.-midnight at 25p.
Piccadilly Bowl, 30 Shaftesbury Avenue, W1 (01-437-1580). Open 10.30 a.m.-6.00 p.m. Children 17p
plus 8p for shoes, adults 27p plus 8p for shoes. From
6.00 p.m.-midnight, 37p. Prices are for a single game.

Trampolining: Best learnt at the *Crystal Palace Sports
Centre. (01-778-0131).*

DO-IT-YOURSELF

This is a do-it-yourself chapter for following up your interests and hobbies. We have tracked down clubs and theatre workshops, art centres, playgroups and adventure playgrounds for you. We suggest some things to see and others to do. You may be interested in some already, others may appeal to you as you read about them. Join in and see.

ARTS AND CRAFTS

For inspiration you may like to visit the *Craft Centre of Great Britain, 43 Earlham Street, WC2 (01-240-3327)* which exhibits the products of craftsmen, pottery, jewellery, silver glass, collage, weaving, Or the *Craftsmen Potters Association of Great Britain, William Blake House, Marshall Street, W1 (01-437-7605)* to see the best of British pots. You can watch *glass blowing* at *The Glass House, 27 Neal Street, WC2 (01-836-9785)*, but telephone first. If you are over twelve you will be allowed to watch at the *White-*

friar's Glassworks, Tudor Road, Harrow, Middlesex, *(01-427-1527).* It is a fantastically exciting craft to watch, but hot. The major art galleries are mentioned in Museums, but one you might like to visit, which often has exhibitions which are interesting and fun, is the *Whitechapel Art Gallery, Whitechapel High Street, E1 (01-247-1492).*

Camden Arts Centre, Arkwright Road, NW3 (01-435-2643/5224). Open Saturday 10.30 a.m.-12.30,for painting, pottery, sculpture for 7 to 11 year olds. Saturday 2.00-4.00 p.m. multi-media (i.e. printing, painting, drawing) projects for 13-16 years old, or teenage pottery. Open Sundays 10.30 a.m.-12.30 for painting, pottery, sculpture for 6-11 year old children. Enrol at the end of June for the year of three ten-week terms at £10.50, which includes the cost of materials used. The course gets booked up very early, but there are occasional vacancies.

Holiday Arts Centre, Hodford Hall, Hodford Road, NW11. An arts study centre for ages 3½-14, sessions take place during the school holidays. The staff are experienced and well qualified, (to look after the youngest there is a nursery school teacher) and lead activities in painting, drawing, drama, ballet, movement, printing and modelling. A Session of nine mornings cost £8.50, including materials. Information from *Mrs. R. Urdang. 132 Willifield Way, NW11 (01-455-6930)* between 9.00 a.m. and 1.00 p.m.

Chelsea Pottery, 13 Radnor Walk, SW3 (01-352-1366) A pottery studio run on a club basis which welcomes children on Saturdays. Morning sessions from 10.00 a.m.-1.00 p.m., afternoons 2.00-5.00 p.m. It is a very friendly group and they make some superb things. A year's subscription is £4.00 for a child, £7.35 for an adult, and £10.00 for the whole family. The charge for each session is 50p. Clay is 3p a lb.

Miss S. Meyer-Michael, 99 North End Road, NW11 (01-455-0817). Miss Meyer-Michael runs pottery classes on Saturday mornings and during the holidays and charges £1.25 for each session of two hours which includes the price of materials and refreshments. During the holidays she runs a special multi-media class for sculpture, painting, modelling and macram. Five-day course costs £7.50. She encourages children to take a pride in their work, and likes them to finish their work so that they can use what they have made.

Children's Art at the End House, 20 Malcolm Road, Wimbledon, SW19 (01-946-2748). Diane White takes children aged 5-17 for art courses during the holidays and on Saturday mornings. A wide variety of art activities include painting, modelling, collage, puppet-making and wire sculpture. A course of 12 lessons including the cost of materials is £5.00.

Sunday Mirror National Exhibition of Children's Art. You will be too late to enter your works for this year's exhibition of work by children under 17. But the show is worth visiting in September or October. Details from *Sunday Mirror National Exhibition of Children's Art, 79 Camden Road, London, NW1 9NT.* Start work for next year now.

BRASS RUBBING

Many churches have brass pictures set in the stone floors. Before you decide to take a rubbing, you must first ask permission from the Rector or Church warden. In some churches, you may be asked to pay a small fee. You will need a roll of paper, (ceiling paper will do), a stick of heelball from a cobbler, a soft nailbrush, a duster and some weights, hassocks do well. Make sure the brass is dusted before you unroll the paper over it, and weight down the corners. Rub the paper gently with the nailbrush first, then, using the flat of the heelball, rub carefully and evenly all over the brass.

Victorian manhole covers are good rubbing material too, and to be found in many a pavement if you look.

BOOKS AND LIBRARIES

Your local library does not just deal out books, it is also a useful source of information. It will have lists of local activities planned for the holidays, and often organizes some itself. In one borough last summer, the libraries held sessions where you could paint, draw, play chess or draughts, do origami, join a stamp club, make a collage, play scrabble, listen to a story, act make a magazine, compete in a quiz and a poetry competition. Not all at once of course, and not in the same library, but find out what yours offers.

Meet your favourite author at the *Children's Bookshow* held in November in the Horticultural Hall, and at Penquin's annual *Exhibition of Puffin Books* in April or May at the *National Book League, 7 Albemarle Street, W1*. Details in Puffin Post, or if you are not a member, write to *Penguin Books Ltd, Bath Road, Harmondsworth, Middlesex* for details.

The Children's Book Centre, 140 Kensington Church Street, W8 (01-229-9646). Authors sometimes tell stories here, but even without them, it is a marvellous place to go and browse. The staff will help you choose a book from the many hundreds available. They have a marvellous stock of paperbacks, and lots of good reference books too. A good shop to send your parents or godparents to if they suggest they might buy you a present.

THEATRES

There are always plays and pantomimes for children at Christmas, but during the rest of the year they are pretty thin on the ground. Two theatres which are specifically for children are:

Unicorn Theatre Club, Arts Theatre, 6 Great Newport Street, WC2 (01-836-7541). This is a club for children who are interested in the theatre. They present plays for different age groups between 4-12 years old, and arrange improvisation sessions, film and puppet shows on Saturday mornings and during the holidays. They provide good teas for parties of children too.

Little Angel Marionette Theatre, 14 Dagmar Passage, Cross Street, N1 (01-226-1787). Marvellous puppet shows for children of 7 and over, with special morning shows for pre-school age children.

The following theatres are worth watching as they occasionally present plays for children:

The Young Vic, The Cut, Waterloor, SE1 (01-928-7616) They run a mailing list club for advance information, priority bookings, and the occasional special performance. The charge is 40p annually.

Mermaid Theatre, Puddle Dock, EC4 (01-236-9521). The molecule club presents seasons of plays for children.

Shaw Theatre, 109 Euston Road, NW1 (01-388-1394).

Royal Court Theatre, The Theatre Upstairs. Sloane Square, SW1 (01-730-5174).

THEATRE WORKSHOPS

Group 64 Youth Theatre, 203b Upper Richmond Road, SW15 (01-788-6943). 7-15 year olds are involved in theatrical activities, puppet making, playwriting, improvisation and fun on Saturday mornings for 50p. a term.

Greenwich Young People's Theatre, Stage Centre, Burrage Road, Plumstead, SE18 (01-854-1316). "Locomotion" is a drama and integrated workshop for children of 7-14 years old. 7-10 year olds can come on Tuesday and Thursday evenings. 11-14 year olds on Saturday mornings. There is a youth theatre for those over 14 for drama, photography, design, etc.

Curtain Theatre Club, Commercial Street, E1 (01-247-6788). A Junior Theatre Club for 7-12 year olds for Saturday morning sessions from 10.30 a.m.-12.30, where you can improvise, paint, make puppets at 2p a session.

Mountview Arts Centre Ltd, 104 Crouch Hill, N8 (01-340-5885). Mountview Theatre School and Club provide theatrical activities for children on Saturday mornings. There are two groups, 6-8 year olds and 8-12 year olds for £2.50 a term.

Oval House Theatre Club, Kennington Oval, SE11 (01-735-2786). This is a creative theatre workshop for children during the holidays.

The Questors, Mattock Lane, Ealing, W5 (01-567-5184). Junior workshops for three age groups, a drama play group for 5-9 year olds, an under-14 Club for 10-13 year olds and Junior Drama Workshop for 14 year olds, at 5p per session, 50p a year and £1.50 a year respectively. The groups are run in a relaxed and informal manner, but a high standard of punctuality and attendance is expected.

Theatre Royal, Stratford East, E15 (01-534-0310). Joan Littlewood's famous theatre workshop where children are welcome on Saturday mornings. After three visits they become members, and are expected to attend regularly so that the group can get to work well together. During the holidays, activities from 10.00 a.m. include drama, fun-making, games and music. Ages from 7 to 17.

Royal Court Theatre, Sloane Square SW1 (01-730-5174). This theatre runs a theatre workshop for children at the *School Hall, St. Michael's Church of England School, Graham Terrace, SW1,* for 11-14 year olds on Tuesday afternoons between 4.15 p.m. and 5.45 p.m. to join contact Joan Mills.

Children's Theatre Workshop, 10 Bulstrode Place, W1. (01-935-7896). Groups of children from 8-16 years old meet for a drama workshop, painting and puppetry. Sometimes they take groups to Dartington Hall for weekend workshops during the holidays.

Roundhouse, Chalk Farm Road, NW6 (01-267-2564). A theatre workshop for children on Saturday mornings between 11.00 a.m. and noon. Special shows and plays in the theatre too.

National Youth Theatre, 81 Eccleston Square, SW1. (01-834-1085). This theatre holds auditions for teenagers who are interested in stage design, lighting and management, as well as for potential actors.

The Local Council Social Services Department may well organize dramatic activities in your district.

MUSIC

All children's concerts are very popular and you must book well in advance.

Royal Festival Hall, South Bank, SE1 (01-928-3191) Write to the organizers for details.

The Robert Mayer Concert Society, 22 Blomfield Street, EC2 (01-588-4714), organise a season of seven concerts during October until March.

The Ernest Read Music Association, 143 King Henry's Road, NW3 (01-722-9644) also run a season of seven concerts.

Fairfield Hall, Croydon, Surrey (01-688-9291) presents concerts for children on Saturday mornings. They are arranged by Arthur Davidson. There are also film shows for children at this theatre.

Royal Albert Hall, Kensington Gore, SW7 (01-598-8212). Sunday concerts promoted by *Victor Hockhauser, 4 Holland Park Avenue, W11 (01-727-0781)* and featuring the top of the classical pops are a good introduction to concert going. Light music and folk concerts are also held at the Royal Albert Hall, but pop has been banished.

For pop concerts it is best to consult the Melody Maker, but regular concerts are held at the *Sundown, Silver Street, Edmonton,* the *Rainbow, Seven Sisters Road, Finsbury Park,* the *Crystal Palace Bowl* during the summer, and *Wembley Stadium* for the big crowd pullers, like the Jackson Five and David Cassidy.

If you want to join the crowd at *Top of the Pops,* or watch any other favourite TV shows live, contact *The Ticket Office, BBC, Portland Place, W1 (01-580-4468), The Ticket Office, ATV, Great Cumberland Place, W1, (01-262-8040),* or *The Ticket Office, Granada Television, 36 Golden Square, W1 (01-734-8080).* During the summer you can join the crowds for concerts in the London Parks, details in the local press and on the gates. Battersea features folk, jazz and steel bands as well as orchestral music on Saturday and Sunday evenings at 7.30 p.m. For military music and brass bands go to Regent's Park, Green Park and the Victoria Embankment Gardens.

OPERA

The Royal Opera House, Covent Garden, WC2 (01-240-1066) and the *Sadlers Wells Opera Company, The*

Coliseum, St. Martin's Lane, WC2 (01-836-3161). (See under Ballet for further details of the Royal Opera House).

BALLET AND DANCING

For performances by the leading ballet companies there are four theatres.

The Royal Opera House, Covent Garden, WC2 (01-240-1066) is the home of the Royal Ballet. For £2.00 a year you can join the Young Friends of the Friends of Covent Garden, and be sent details of performances, get discounts on tickets, and be allowed to attend some dress rehearsals.

The Royal Festival Hall, South Bank, SE1 (01-928-3191) presents the London Festival Ballet which also dances at the *Sadlers Wells Theatre, Rosebery Avenue, EC1 (01-837-1672).* You can see visiting ballets here too.

The Jeanetta Cochrane Theatre, Southampton Row, WC1 (01-242-7040) is the home of the Ballet Rambert.

The Royal Academy of Dancing, 48 Vicarage Crescent, SW11 (01-223-0091), or the *Imperial Society of Teachers of Dancing, 70 Gloucester Place, W1 (01-935-0825)* will send you details of schools and names of teachers if you want to dance yourself.

The Folk Dance and Song Festival is held at the Albert Hall in February, and visiting troupes perform here too.

CINEMA

The Odeon and ABC Cinemas have Saturday morning performances. *The ICA, Nash House, The Mall, SW1, (01-930-6393(* show children's films on Saturday and Sunday afternoons at 3.00 p.m. for 25p.

Cartoon cinemas are fast vanishing, but there are two, one in Piccadilly, the other in Victoria Station.

PLAY

There is lots of action in playgrounds all over London. Some are run by local councils, others by voluntary workers, others by private Play schemes. Your local library, Citizen's Advice Bureau, or Social Services Department of the local council will give you information. So will *The Children & Youth Action Group, "Make Children Happy", 16 North End Road, Golder's Green, NW11 (01-455-6755)* who are compiling a list of play schemes and centres.

The GLC run *1 O'Clock Clubs* for toddlers and their mothers in the GLC Parks. Activities include painting, modelling, sand and water play and story time. They also organise Community Play Centres, Play Parks and Adventure Playgrounds, which provide facilities for all sorts of activities, art pottery, films and adventure areas for building things.

Play Space, 68 Claylands Road, Oval, SW8 (01-735-9094) is a new organisation whose play leaders include adventure playground leaders, teachers, psychiatrists and students. At present they make up four teams which operate in the Croydon area, Southwark, Victoria and the West End. They work with children and adults, recruiting them from the street, to join in sessions of intensive play which might be film-making, drama and improvisation. Contact *Lawrence Butler (01-636-8514)* or *(01-794-6650)* who also runs Play Workshops once a month for adults interested in the scheme.

The Camden Council of Social Service, 25 Euston Road, NW1 (01-8370-2793) run four adventure playgrounds in the area. *Park Hill Playground, Park Hill Road, W3; Chester Road Playground, Raydon Street, N19; Peckwater Estate Playground, Islip Street, NW5* and *Plot 10, Summerstown, Polygon Road, NW1.*

The London Adventure Playground Association, 57b Catherine Place, SW1 (01-834-0656) will give you details of the adventure playgrounds where you can build huts and forts, light fires and cook, climb trees, dig holes, camp, dress up, in fact "do your own thing". Playleaders are in charge to help if needed.

MODEL RAILWAY AND TRANSPORT ENTHUSIASTS

The Malden and District Society of Model Engineers, Claygate Lane, Thames Ditton, Surrey (01-398-3985). Visitors are welcome and may ride on the steam trains they lovingly construct and maintain. You can see round the workshops and examine the many superb models. Open on the first Sunday in every month from Easter to October inclusive, and on Easter, Whitsun and August Bank Holiday Mondays.

Syon House houses the London Transport Collection and "History on Wheels". (See Jaunts).

Veteran Car Club, London-Brighton Rally. Held on the first Sunday in November these marvellous old cars set off for Brighton from Hyde Park Corner at 8.00 a.m.

BOATING, LAKES AND DINOSAURS TOO

which may seem an odd combination, but exists.

Crystal Palace Park, SE26. (01-778-7148). Lurking in the trees and bushes, surrounding the lake, is a very lifelike collection of prehistoric monsters, mostly reptiles, which were made in 1853. At a party to cele-brate their completion 21 people sat down to dinner inside Iguanadon. All this and rowing too! The boating lake is open daily from Easter to October, and weekends only during the winter. A boat for four costs 50p an hour, with a 50p deposit. The Park houses a small zoo as well, so you should find plenty to do here.

Regent's Park, NW1. Two boating lakes here, one for children only, the other for children over 14, or accompanied by their parents. The shallow lake has motorboats, paddleboats and canoes for hire, all of which can be managed safely by young children. Open mid March-November, depending on the weather from 10.00 a.m.-½ hour before the park closes. A motorboat for one will cost 14p for 20 minutes. The other, deeper lake is open from March-October depending on the weather. 25p for a single skiff with 25p deposit. 35p for a rowing boat for four with a 35p deposit. Four children's playgrounds here, which have puppet shows twice daily during the summer, for one week at each. Boating in Battersea Park (see Parks and Palaces), and the Serpentine (ditto), at Bushey Park, Hampton Court, and at Greenwich Park. For serious rowing see Sports. For river trips and canals see Jaunts.

WINDMILLS

Apart from the well-known working models of windmills in the Science Museum, there are three mills in the London area for you to examine.

Brixton, The Tower Mill in Blenheim Gardens. Built in 1816, many of the timbers are ships timbers and considerably older than the mill itself. It was restored with new sails and machinery taken from a mill in Lincolnshire. Ask the park attendant to let you see it. Admission 5p.

Smockmill, St. Mary's Lane, Upminster. This was built in 1803. Now repaired and preserved, it is the largest complete smockmill in the Eastern counties. Much of the machinery is in place although the shutters have been taken from the sails, and are stored inside. If you are interested you can write to the Town Clerk, London Borough of Havering, Romford, Essex, enclosing a sae for permission to view.

Wimbledon Common Mill. Although it is not open to the public, you can view it very closely. It is a composite mill. The lower part, which once housed the machinery, is now a house, but the sails still turn above.

NATURALISTS AND BIRDWATCHERS

After visiting the Natural History Museum, the Horniman Museum and the Zoo, you may want to see what London's Parks have to offer.

Wimbledon and Putney Commons. (01-788-7655). This is one of the few remaining places in the country where no pesticides have been used and where a policy of natural regeneration is followed. If a tree falls. down it is left alone, if a ditch should become blocked, it is left blocked and the land around it naturally becomes boggy. Consequently it is a splendid place for birds and insects. You might even catch a glimpse of a womble if you keep your eyes skinned.

Richmond Park is the home of badgers, foxes, deer and masses of birds; a crested grebe is often on Pen Ponds.

St. James's Park, Kew Gardens, Syon Park are good for ducks and geese, some of them quite rare. If you are accompanied by an accredited adult birdwatcher, 14-17 year olds can watch birds on the reservoirs. Write to *The Clerk of the Board, Metropolitan Water Board, 173 Rosebery Avenue, EC1.*

Hampstead Heath is a great expanse of wilderness to walk in, with several ponds, and super views of London if you get bored with watching wildlife.

FISHING

London Anglers' Association, 32 Stroud Green Road, Finsbury Park N4 (01-263-0196) will give you details of clubs and places to fish. You can try to catch the roach, tench, carp, pike, bream, gudgeon, perch and eels which live in London's ponds and river. No permit is required to fish the river between Richmond and Staines, or to fish in the GLC Parks during the season 16th June-14th March; ponds in Battersea Park, Clissold Park, Eagle Park, Clapham Common, Finsbury Park, Hampstead Heath, Tooting Common and Victoria Park. Apply for a free permit from the *Park Superintendent, Hampton Court, and Bushey Parks, Middlesex,* to fish in the Long Water and Richmond Ponds at Hampton Court Park, and in the Leg of Mutton, Diana and Heron Ponds in Bushey Park. Apply to the *Park Superintendent, Hyde Park, W2,* for the Serpentine and Osterley Park, and to the *Park Superintendent, Richmond Park, Surrey,* for Pen Ponds, Richmond Park.

CONSUMER COUNSEL

There are specialist shops throughout London for children's clothes, toys and hobbies. Obviously this cannot be a comprehensive list of them, so we have chosen those we know personally, or which have been recommended to us. We include a list of restaurants in which to revive the exhausted shophounds and hopefully there will be one to suit your mood and pocket in the right district. Eating out with very young children is best avoided in our experience, but if you must take the baby too, choose a restaurant marked with an asterisk, which means high chairs are provided, and not too many pained looks thrown in your direction if the food starts flying. Most of the big department stores have quiet restaurants, together with children's clothes departments for the school uniform agonies, and they are usually the best bet for lavatories.too.

*Harrods Ltd. Knightsbridge, SW1 (01-730-1234)
You could keep a child happily occupied in Harrods

for hours. There is an excellent toy department and children's books, a zoo if you want to buy a pet or just look at the exotic stock, a music and record department, sports goods, art materials, jigsaws, needlework department and escalators connecting them all. There are good clothes for babies, up to 7 years old, a boys' department and a good selection for girls of all ages, including the difficult to find 11 to 14 years old. The hairdressing department is very good, with a rocking horse as bait, and there is a restaurant. Way-In for teenage gear, accessories, records, posters, huge photos of yourself, snack bar and lovely loud music. *Peter Jones, Sloane Square, SW1 (01-730-3434),* has good clothes and the best children's shoe department in London. *Dickens and Jones, Regent Street, W1. (01-734-7070)* for clothes and next door *Liberty and Co. Ltd, Regent Street, W1 (01-734-1234)* for lovely materials and dresses smocked to delight Granny and Nanny.

For the latest gear and good cheap bright clothes, search the *Kensington Market, 49 Kensington High Street, W8 (01-937-7480). The Great Gear Trading Co. Ltd, 85 Kings Road, SW3 (02-352-3168)* and *Biba, 124 Kensington High Street, W8 (01-937-6287)* who are shortly moving across the road to take over the Derry and Toms building when they will extend their children's clothes and toy department. For ex-service clothes and equipment, belts, hats, knives, jeans and anoraks try *Laurence Corner, 62-64 Hampstead Road, NW1 (01-387-6134)* or *Millett's, 89, Oxford Street, W1 (01-437-2811).* For boys and girls who live in jeans. the best shop of all is *Colts, 414 Richmond Road, East Twickenham (01-892-1553)* and at *5 Hampstead Road, NW3 (01-435-7387).* They do an excellent mail order service too. *Orange Hand, 11 Golder's Green Road, NW11 (01-455-2393)* and at *Sloane Square, SW1 (01-730-5098),* stock a good range of tough clothes at nice cheap prices and they do mail order too. For girls (up to 11) *Pollyanna, 35 Thayer Street, W1 (01-936-4739)* and *660 Fulham Road, SE6 (01-731-0673)* have a lovely collection of things, also for boys and some for babies. They do mail order as well. For the sisters of Colts customers, *Darling Daughters, 61 South End Road, NW3 (01-435-0236)* is especially good for 10 year olds up, (usually hard to find) as well as their younger sisters.

Don't forget *The Scotch House, 2 Brompton Road, SW1 (01-589-4421)* for sweaters and kilts, *Little Horrors, Cheval Place, SW7 (01-589-5289), Little Things, 21 Beauchamp Place, SW3 (01-589-8563), Small Wonder, 296a Kings Road, SW3 (01-352-9608)* and *Wizard of Oz, 42 Edith Grove, SW10 (01-351-2804)* are good hunting grounds for younger children. If money is no object, *The Rocking Horse Ltd, 167 Sloane Street, SW1 (01-235-3334)* has fabulous things, so does *Mome, 66 Fulham Road, SW3 (01-584-9321).* At the other end of the financial scale and not to be missed are, obviously, *Marks and Spencer Ltd, C & A Modes* and *British Home Stores,* with all the *Mothercare branches* for babies' things.

TOY SHOPS

There are usually good toy departments in the big stores. *Harrods* is particularly good, *Selfridges* is big and brash. *Heal's* is very design conscious, *Hamley Bros. Ltd, 200 Regent Street, W1 (01-734-3161)* is the biggest toy shop in town with four packed floors. Why we can never find what we want remains a mystery. In central London, *Paul and Marjorie Abbatt Ltd, 74 Wigmore Street, W1 (01-487-1382)* and *James Galt & Co. Ltd, 30 Great Marlborough Street (01-734-0829)* are both pioneers in creative play, with marvellously made toys and lots of helpful advice. Galts have good clay too. *Pollocks Toy Museum, 1 Scala Street, W1. (01-636-3452)* is a fascinating little shop with wooden peg dolls, theatres and gingerbread men to buy and eat. *John Dobbie, 79 Wimbledon High Street, SW19*

(01-946-7981) is run by parents of a large family. They are very helpful and have wonderful things from large climbing frames to pocket money toys for a few pence. *Tridias, 44 Monmouth Street, WC2 (01-240-2369)* and at *Sheen Road, Richmond (01-948-3459)* have a marvellous selection of things, kites and lots of stocking-filler type toys, so do *The Owl and the Pussycat, 11 Flask Walk, NW3 (01-435-5342). Where .the Wild Things are, Mortlake Terrace, Kew (010940-8223)* is a fascinating little shop with the most covetable doll in London, a copy of a Victorian one with a really pretty face and gorgeous clothes, among many other things, *Laffeaty's, 345 Kings Road, SW1 (01-352-2705)* is a happy hunting ground especially for boys, with masses of model soldiers and model railway equipment. Don't forget *W.H. Smiths, Boots,* or the *British Home Stores.*

For Playroom emergencies there is the *Doll's Hospital, 16 Dawes Road, SW6 (01-385-2081)* which will restore almost any doll to health and *Beatties, 112 High Holborn, WC1 (01-405-6285)* will do the same for cars, train sets and broken engines. They also have a good stock of new and second hand cars and trains.

BOOKSHOPS

The Children's Book Centre, 140 Kensington Church Street, W8 (01-229-9646) has the best selection of books in London and is the best possible place to take your book tokens. They have reference books, picture books, paperbacks and good advice too. *The Owl and the Pussycat* (see Toys) have a good selection. *Harrods, Foyles, 119 Charing Cross Road, WC2 (01-437-5660)* and *Hatchards Ltd, 187 Piccadilly, W1 (01-734-1072)* all have children's books. The *Beauchamp Children's Bookshop, 36 Beauchamp Place, SW3 (01-589-7816)* has few paperbacks, but there is a good choice otherwise.

HOBBIES

Every district has a shop selling balsa wood and glue, but our favourite is *J & D Hobbies, 118a Upper Richmond Road, SW15 (01-788-6497)* for everything to do with model-making and leather. *The Hobby Horse Ltd, 17 Langton Street, SW10 (01-351-1913)* has equipment and advice for any amount of hobbies. *The Needlewoman Shop, 146 Regent Street, W1 (01-734-1727)* and *Harrods* are the best places for needlework addicts and the *Felt and Hessian Shop, 35 Greville Street, EC1* is good for these two materials. *Windsor and Newton, 51 Rathbone Place, W1 (01-636-4231)* are specialists in paint and art materials. For paper, mounting card, sheets of acetate, or paper decorations go to *F.G. Kettle, 127 High Holborn, WC1 (01-405-9764)* or to *Paperchase, 216 Tottenham Court Road, W1 (01-637-1121)* which has posters and Gorgeous wrapping paper too. *Partymad, 67 Gloucester Avenue, London NW1* is the place for brilliant paper plates and party invitations, including inflatable ones, most of them imported from America.

Phillips and Page, 50 Kensington Church Street, W8 (01-937-5859) stock brass rubbing equipment. Go to *Kodak, 63 Kingsway, WC2 (01-405-7841)* for everything photographic, while *HMV, 363 Oxford Street, W1 (01-629-1240)* has an enormous stock of records. If you are looking for folk or jazz, go to *Dobell's, 75/77 Charing Cross Road, WC2 (01-437-5746/3075), Lillywhite's Lower Regent Street, SW1 (01-930-3181)* is renowned for sporting equipment, you can get camping equipment at *Benjamin Edgington, 29 Queen Elizabeth Street, SE1 (01-407-3734)* and at *Pindisports, 14 Holborn, EC1 (01-242-3278)*.

For collectors of shells, minerals, rocks and associated geological things, *Gemrocks, 7 Holborn, EC1 (01-242-7725)* and, surprisingly, there is also a good selection at *The Eaton Bag Co, Ltd, 16 Manette Street, W1 (01-437-9391)*. Stamp collectors should go to *Stanley Gibbons Ltd, 391 Strand, WC2 (01-836-9707)*. Pet hops abound throughout London but two of our favourites are *Animal Fair, 17 Abingdon Road, W8 (01-937-0011)* and the *Regent Pet Stores, 35 Parkway, NW1 (01-485-5163)* and don't forget *Harrod's Zoo,* Go to the *RSPCA* and *Battersea Dogs' Home* for strays.

FOOD

We asked dozens of children where they liked to eat in London and every other one said *The Great American Disaster, 9 Beauchamp Place, SW3 (01-589-0992)* and *335 Fulham Road, SW10 (01-351-1188)*. Be prepared for queues at peak times but it is worth the wait for delicious Hamburgers, chicken and ice-cream. Of the same type *The Hard Rock Cafe, 50 Old Park Lane, W1 (01-493-1923)* is popular too, so is *The Great American Success, 100 Kensington High Street, W8 (01-937-0257)*. Go to *Asterix, 329 Kings Road, SW3 (01-352-3891)* for superb pancakes, and the *Ice-Dream Parlour, Fulham Road, SW10* opposite The Great American Disaster, for 40 different varieties of ice cream, and a juke box too. *Pizza Express* and *Pizza Land* have branches throughout London, and *The Spaghetti House, 15 Goodge Street, W1 (01-580-1578)* has branches at *17 Knightsbridge, 4 Hans Road, SW3* and *24 Cranbourn Street, WC2*. *Fortes Quality Inns* have special children's menus, so do the **Old Kentucky* chain of restaurants, who specialise in pancakes and waffles, and give lollipops to children who finish their food. **The Golden Egg* chain of restaurants is good for the egg and chips with everything brigade. *Cranks Salad Table, 8 Marshall Street, W1 (01-437-9431)* for the minority who will eat delicious salads. Chinese and Indian food is very popular, closely followed by Italian. It is worth making the journey to *The Friends, 11 Creed Street, EC4 (01-238-5189); The Good Friends, 139 Salmon Lane, E14 (01-987-5541)* and the *New Friends, 185 Salmon Lane, E14 (01-543-3366)* if you like Cantonese Chinese food.

For Pekingese, try the *Dumpling Inn, 15a Gerrard Street, W1 (01-437-2567)* or the *Richmond Rendezvous, 1 Paradise Road, Richmond (01-940-5114). Kwality, 145 Whitfield Street, W1 (01-387-6767)* is one of the best of the many Indian restaurants. You can usually judge the standard of these by the number of Indians who are eating there. *Chea Ciccio, 38c. Kensington Church Street, W8 (01-937-2005)* has excellent Italian food. The last seven restaurants mentioned are open for lunch on Sundays, but it is always wise to check first.

For restaurants charging less than £1 per head and also open on Sundays for lunch, try the following. *Schmidt's 33-43 Charlotte Street, W1.(01-636-8932)* is a German restaurant with a wide choice of dishes and constantly mentioned as really good value. *Alpino Restaurants, 3 Lower Grosvenor Place, SW1 (01-839-2929)* have good Italian and Swiss/German food. Try the *Casserole, 67 Tottenham Court Road, W1 (01-636-1099)* which is very good and very cheap. For Turkish food go to *Jimmy's, 24 Frith Street, W1.* and for Polish food try *Daquise, 20 Thurloe Street, SW7 (01-589-6117). The Haymarket Room, 18-19 Coventry Street, W1 (01-734-9786)* is open 24 hours a day, all week, for jacket potatoes with interesting fillings.

For impromptu picnics, take-away food is a blessing. There are over 30 branches of the *Kentucky Fried Chicken House,* fish-and-chip shops are everywhere, and you can take away Chinese food from many places including the *Chinese Barbecue Shop, 22 Earlham Street, WC2 (01-836-6107).*

Tea seems to be a dying meal, but for those given to indulging in a little something about 4.00 p.m., there are various branches of the *Fuller's tea shops. Kenco Coffee Houses* and *J. Lyons & Company Ltd.* are two other tea-time institutions. The *Ceylon Tea Centre, 22 Regent Street, W1* is as good for tea as its name implies. For especially delicious affairs, try

Bendicks either at *55 Wigmore Street, W1* or at *40 New Bond Street.* Another very exotic place for afternoon tea is *Gloriette, 128 Brompton Road, SW3* (opposite Harrods) where they serve the most delicious patisserie.

MARKETS

Markets are great fun, not just for the bargains you may pick up, but for the people, the noise and the general atmosphere. People have been trading in the streets since the City's earliest beginnings and some of the Markets have been held for hundreds of years. You must get up very early to visit the three most exciting wholesale food markets.

Billingsgate, Lower Thames Street, EC3.

Tube: Monument. Open from 5.30 a.m. daily.

Get there around 6.00 a.m. for marvellous fishy smells and the sight of fish gleaming silver in their boxes. The porters wear special flat hats made of leather and wood and the pavements run wet with sluicing water. You might almost be in a fishing town on the coast.

Smithfield, Charterhouse Street, EC1.

Tube: Farringdon. Open from 6.00 a.m. daily.

Smithfield was once famous for its fairs. The medieval horse fair 'Bartholomew Fair', was held here annually until the 19th century. It is now the largest meat market in the world.

Covent Garden, WC2.

Tube: Covent Garden. Most interesting about 6.00 a.m. daily. Closed on Saturdays.

You must go to Covent Garden soon for the market

is being moved to a new site at Nine Elms in the near future. It is the principal market in London for flowers, fruit and vegetables. The Floral Hall blazes with flowers and the smell is delicious. The market is packed with lorries and porters struggle through the crowds laden with country produce. There are many cafes in and around all three markets where you can get a good breakfast. A visit to one of these would make a good start to a day's sightseeing.

Portobello Road, Notting Hill, W11.

Tube: Ladbrooke Grove, Notting Hill. Open on Saturdays only.

This is a world-famous market for antiques, bric-a-brac, old clothes, silver, in fact almost anything is sold here at dozens of small stalls. Great fun to watch the crowds even if you don't buy anything.

Petticoat Lane, Middlesex Street, E1.

Tube: Liverpool Street. Open on Sundays only from 9.00 a.m. to 2.00 p.m.

Everything is sold here, clothes, bric-a-brac, seafood, all from a great complex of stalls.

Caledonian Market, Tower Bridge Road, Bermondsey, SE1.

Tube: London Bridge. Open on Fridays from 10.00 a.m. to 4.00 p.m.

Here there are mostly antiques which you may find next morning at Portobello Road.

Club Row, Sclater Street, E1.

Tube: Shoreditch. Open on Sundays from 8.00 a.m. to 1.00 p.m.

The principal pet market for animals, birds, fish

and reptiles, it is kept under the watchful eye of the RSPCA.

Camden Passage, Islington High Street, N1.

Tube: Angel. Open Wednesdays and Saturdays from 9.00 a.m. to 6.00 p.m.

Here you can buy antiques and watch the crowds examining them.

Chelsea Antique Market, 252 Kings Road, SW3.

Tube: Sloane Square. Open daily from 10.00 a.m. to 6.00 p.m. but not on Monday afternoons.

Aquarius, Kings Road, SW3.

Tube: Sloane Square.

This is very much the same type of place as Chelsea Antique Market.

London Silver Vaults, Chancery House, Chancery Lane, WC2.

Tube: Chancery Lane. Open Monday to Friday 9.30 a.m. to 5.30 p.m., Saturdays 9.30 a.m. to 12.30 p.m.

Not really a market, but the largest collection of silver in the world, and well worth a visit.

CALENDAR

We have listed the year's main events and exhibitions in the months in which they usually occur. Some exhibitions vary from year to year, both as to time and place, so it is wiser to check first. Royal Birthdays are given so that you will know when to dash off to Hyde Park or the Tower to watch the Gun Salutes in their honour.

JANUARY

International Racing Car Show at Olympia.
International Holiday Exhibition at Olympia.
Model Engineering Exhibition at Seymour Hall.
International Boat Show at Earl's Court.

FEBRUARY

6th: Anniversary of the Queen's Accession.
Crufts Dog Show at Olympia.
Festival of Folk Song and Dance at the Royal Albert Hall.
Chinese New Year, processions and dancing in the streets of Soho.

MARCH

London Dinghy Exhibition at the Crystal Palace Sports Centre.
Head of the River Race - Mortlake.
Oxford and Cambridge Boat Race Putney-Mortlake. (Sometimes in April).

EASTER

River and Canal trips, most boating lakes launch their operations.
Battersea Festival Gardens and Funfair opens.
Easter Parade at Battersea Festival Gardens.

Chessington Zoo and Circus in full swing.
Shell Public Viewing Gallery opens.
Fairs on Hampstead Heath, Blackheath and Wormwood Scrubs.

APRIL

21st: Queen's Birthday (unofficial).
Puffin Book Show at National Book League.
Physics Exhibition at Earl's Court.

MAY

29th: Founders Day at the Royal Hospital Chelsea.
FA Cup Final - Wembley.
Chelsea Flower Show.
Beating Retreat on Horseguards.
Rehearsals for Trooping the Colour on Horseguards.
Fair on Lower Common Putney.

WHITSUN

Fairs on Hampstead Heath, Blackheath, Wormwood Scrubs.

JUNE

2nd: Queen's Official Birthday.
6th: Derby Day at Epsom.
10th: Prince Philip's Birthday.
Royal Ascot.
Trooping the Colour on Horseguards.
Beating Retreat on Horseguards.
Test Match at Lords.
Wimbledon Lawn Tennis Championships.
Festival of London.
Service at St. Paul's, Bedford Street, Covent Garden to bless pets and animals.
Royal Academy Summer Exhibition.

JULY

Royal Tournament at Earl's Court with the march
past in Battersea Park the weekend before.
Doggetts Coat and Badge Race.
Swan Upping.
Promenade Concerts at the Royal Albert Hall.
Royal International Horse Show at Wembley.

AUGUST

4th: Queen Mother's Birthday
International Handicrafts and Do-It-Yourself exhibi-
tion at Olympia.
Greater London Horse Show at Clapham Common.
Test Match at the Oval.

SEPTEMBER

Cricket Gillette Cup Finals at Lords.
Sunday Mirror Exhibition of Children's Art.
Arthur Davidson season of children's concerts begin
at Fairfield Hall, Croydon.

OCTOBER

International Motor Show at Earl's Court.
National Brass Band Championship at the Royal Albert
Hall.
Cenotaph Service on Remembrance Sunday.
Ernest Read and Robert Meyer season of children's
concerts begin at the Festival Hall.

NOVEMBER

First Sunday Veteran Car Club's London-Brighton
Rally from Hyde Park Corner.
Lord Mayor's Show.
Children's Book Show at the Horticultural Hall.
International Camping and Caravan Exhibition at Earl's
Court.

DECEMBER

National Cat Championships at Olympia.
Richmond Championship Dog Show at Olympia.
Smithfield Show at Earl's Court.
Caged Bird's Show at Alexandra Palace.

Some Useful Addresses.

Olympia, Kensington, W14. (01-603-3344)
Earl's Court, Exhibition Building SW5. (01-385-1200).
Horticultural, Hall, Vincent Square, SW1. (01-834-4333)
Seymour Hall, Seymour Street, W1.
Empire Stadium Wembley, Empire Way, Wembley.
    (01-902-1234).
Crystal Palace Sports Centre, SE19. (01-778-0131).
Central Hall, Storey's Gate, SW1.(01-930-4259).
Alexandra Palace, N22. (01-883-9711).
Royal Albert Hall, Kensington Gore, SW7.(01-598-
    8212).
Royal Festival Hall, South Bank, SE1.(01-928-
    3191).
The Fairfield Hall, Croydon. (01-688-9291).

110

111